A Texas
Trilogy

A Texas Trilogy

Preston Jones

*The Last Meeting of the
Knights of the White Magnolia*

Lu Ann Hampton Laverty Oberlander

The Oldest Living Graduate

A Mermaid Dramabook

 HILL AND WANG • NEW YORK
A division of Farrar, Straus and Giroux

Published simultaneously in Canada by
McGraw-Hill Ryerson Ltd., Toronto
Second printing, 1978
Designed by Gustave Niles

Library of Congress Cataloging in Publication Data

Jones, Preston.
A Texas trilogy.

(A Mermaid dramabook)
CONTENTS: The last meeting of the Knights of the
White Magnolia.—Lu Ann Hampton Laverty Oberlander.—
The oldest living graduate.
I. Title.
PS3560.05244T4 1976   812'.5'4   76–42982
ISBN 0–8090–9183–6
ISBN 0–8090–1236–7 pbk.

To my beloved wife, Mary Sue

Author's Note

An extraordinary energy in the theater is the energy of the playwright. It tells us things. It gives us life as no other element of theater can. It is relentless and often difficult. So, pay attention.

PAUL BAKER

For a playwright, there can be no greater thrill than to see his plays first come to life on the stage. Therefore, I look back with special fondness to the fall of 1973 when the Dallas Theater Center began work on *A Texas Trilogy*. As a member of the Theater Center since 1962, I had come to appreciate the hard work and lively creativity that surround each production. This became especially clear to me when the trilogy plays were produced under the direction of Paul Baker.

The Dallas Theater Center has a tradition of producing original plays because Paul Baker is committed to supporting the playwright on both artistic and economic levels. My plays, and those of other writers, have grown out of this nourishing atmosphere, one which encourages each new play to find its way.

Rehearsals for *A Texas Trilogy* were creative enterprises involving everyone. Lines were added and cut, plots were

strengthened. Schemes were devised to help actors understand the social and environmental aspects of Bradleyville. In
order to deepen their characterizations, actors were asked to
construct collages designed to capture, in textural forms, the
basic elements of each character's past life. These and other
techniques used throughout rehearsals of the three plays
were valuable and stimulating to all of us—director, de-
signer, actors, and playwright alike.

For this enriching experience I am grateful to Paul Baker,
Eugene McKinney, Randy Moore, Ken Latimer, Sallie Lau-
rie, Mona Pursley, Robyn Flatt, James Crump, John Henson,
Synthia Rodgers, John Logan, Tim Green, William Landrey,
Allen Hibbard, Tommy Kendrick, Ted Mitchell, Sam Nance,
Keith Dixon, Chris McCarty, Charles Beachley, Roger Rich-
ards, Matt Tracy, and Rebecca Ramsey. I wish to acknowl-
edge my appreciation to these fine artists and true first citi-
zens of Bradleyville.

The Last Meeting of the Knights of the White Magnolia was first performed at the Down Center Stage of the Dallas Theater Center on December 4, 1973. Two months later, on February 5, 1974, *Lu Ann Hampton Laverty Oberlander* premiered at the same theater. Then, beginning on November 19, 1974, with *The Oldest Living Graduate*, all three plays were produced in repertory on the Dallas Theater Center's main stage, the Kalita Humphreys Theater. Performances were under the direction of Paul Baker and cast from the resident company and graduate apprentices at the Dallas Theater Center.

The Last Meeting of the Knights of the White Magnolia was chosen by the American Playwrights Theatre as its 1975–76 offering, and the play has been produced by numerous regional, university, civic, and professional theaters across the country.

Starting on April 29, 1976, the John F. Kennedy Center for the Performing Arts presented *A Texas Trilogy* in repertory at its Eisenhower Theater in Washington, D.C. The plays, which ran for a ten-week season under the direction of Alan Schneider, were produced by Robert Whitehead and Roger L. Stevens. On August 5, 1976, the trilogy was brought back to the Kennedy Center for a five-week run prior to its New York opening.

The Robert Whitehead–Roger L. Stevens production, under Alan Schneider's direction, opened at the Broadhurst Theatre in New York City on September 21, 1976, with the following cast:

The Last Meeting of the Knights of the White Magnolia

Ramsey-Eyes	JOHN MARRIOTT
Rufe Phelps	WALTER FLANAGAN
Olin Potts	THOMAS TONER
Red Grover	PATRICK HINES
L. D. Alexander	HENDERSON FORSYTHE
Colonel J. C. Kinkaid	FRED GWYNNE
Skip Hampton	GRAHAM BECKEL
Lonnie Roy McNeil	PAUL O'KEEFE
Milo Crawford	JOSH MOSTEL

Lu Ann Hampton Laverty Oberlander

Claudine Hampton	AVRIL GENTLES
Lu Ann Hampton	DIANE LADD
Billy Bob Wortman	JAMES STALEY
Skip Hampton	GRAHAM BECKEL
Dale Laverty	EVERETT MCGILL

Red Grover	PATRICK HINES
Rufe Phelps	WALTER FLANAGAN
Olin Potts	THOMAS TONER
Corky Oberlander	BAXTER HARRIS
Milo Crawford	JOSH MOSTEL
Charmaine	KRISTIN GRIFFITH

The Oldest Living Graduate

Martha Ann Sickenger	KRISTIN GRIFFITH
Maureen Kinkaid	PATRICIA ROE
Colonel J. C. Kinkaid	FRED GWYNNE
Mike Tremaine	RALPH ROBERTS
Floyd Kinkaid	LEE RICHARDSON
Clarence Sickenger	HENDERSON FORSYTHE
Major Leroy W. Ketchum	WILLIAM LE MASSENA
Cadet Whopper Turnbull	PAUL O'KEEFE
Claudine Hampton	AVRIL GENTLES

(When *A Texas Trilogy* was first performed at the Kennedy Center, the part of Claudine Hampton was played by Kate Wilkinson and Charmaine by Janet Grey.)

Scenery and lighting were by Ben Edwards and costumes by Jane Greenwood.

Contents

A Texas
Trilogy

The Place

Bradleyville, Texas—population 6,ooo—a small, dead West Texas town in the middle of a big, dead West Texas prairie between Abilene and San Angelo. The new highway has bypassed it and now the world is trying to.

The People

THE HAMPTON FAMILY

CLAUDINE HAMPTON attended high school in Bradleyville and, through a program at the hospital, became a practical nurse. She married Lloyd Hampton. Lloyd worked for the refinery until his death in 1945. Claudine has two children, Skip and Lu Ann. Both of them are grown now but still remain a great source of worry to her. Mrs. Hampton is well known in town for her ability and honesty.

SKIP HAMPTON was born and raised in Bradleyville, graduating from high school and serving in the army during the Korean War. In his entire life Skip has never been able to distinguish himself in any type of endeavor. If you look in his *Senior Year Annual* from Bradleyville High, you'll find under his picture the name Skip Hampton and nothing else. During Korea, Skip drove a supply truck—never getting closer to the front than sixty miles; however, with the passage of time and especially after many drinks, his war record gets bloodier and bloodier. After the war Skip tried several get-rich-quick schemes that always melted in his hands. Then he discovered the bottle. Skip is unmarried and lives with his mother and sister. He pumps gas for a living and has finally been able to distinguish himself in the eyes of all Bradleyville. He is the town drunk.

LU ANN HAMPTON was born at the Bradleyville Memorial
Hospital in 1936. She suffered through the usual amount of
bites, cuts, scratches, bruises, and minor childhood ail-
ments, but never knew real heartbreak until her father
died in 1945. Another blow came when her best friend
moved to California in 1947.

Always a popular girl in school, Lu Ann held several offices.
She was co-editor of the grade school *Messenger,* and member of the Pepettes drill team. In high school, she was four
times elected to the student senate as the representative of
Miss Scott's home room and was, in her sophomore year,
Future Farmers of America Sweetheart and class yearbook
reporter. She could have held many more offices, but the
demanding chores of being Head Cheerleader for the past
two years have forced her to curtail many activities. Lu Ann
lives with her mother and brother at 301 Grand Street and
goes steady with Billy Bob Wortman. After graduation from
high school, she plans "to have lots and lots of fun."

CHARMAINE is Lu Ann's daughter by Dale Laverty. After
Corky Oberlander was killed, Lu Ann moved back into her
mother's house and Charmaine was brought up there. She is
spoiled and pampered by her mother, her grandmother, and
her uncle.

Charmaine became the child of an unsettled household
and unsettled times. As the years passed, she grew ashamed
of her mother, contemptuous of her uncle, and utterly unsee-
ing of her invalid grandmother. Her school grades are bad,
her outlook bleak, her lifestyle slovenly and wasteful, but
maybe all these negatives equip her better than her mother
for today's times.

BILLY BOB WORTMAN lives with his mother, father, and three
younger sisters in a small house on Austin Street. Always
interested in agriculture, Billy Bob has been a member of
Future Farmers of America since 1947, and his entries have
won many prizes at the Mumford County Fair. Now, in his
senior year in high school, Billy Bob is an Eagle Scout, a

Y.M.C.A. summer camp counselor, and a starting forward on the varsity basketball team.

Next to his father, Billy Bob considers Reverend Stone of the First Christian Church one of the finest men that ever lived. Billy Bob started going steady with Lu Ann Hampton at the beginning of his senior year, right after she had broken up with Floyd Tatum and he had broken up with Eveline Blair. (Ruthie Lee Lawell got them together at a sockhop.)

Billy Bob isn't too sure what his plans are after graduation, but you can bet whatever it is, it will have something to do with basketball and the Lord.

DALE LAVERTY was born and raised in San Angelo, Texas. Always a big kid, Dale was known as Tubby Rump until he made first-string tackle on the football team and became known as the Hulk.

Dale's father was a truck driver and trucks became the passion of Dale's life. He dreamed of them. He saw himself in the cab rolling along in his own rig, booming across the Western plains, free and easy with the girls at the brightly lit truck stops. He would dream of swinging out of the cab and eating hugely on ham and eggs, great bowls of chili, fat-dripping cheeseburgers, and chicken-fried steak swimming and bubbling in heavy gravy.

Dale would like to be the hood ornament of a Mack truck, solid, heavy, tough, staring down the road in open-eyed defiance.

After the Korean War, in which he served as a truck driver, Dale came home with great goals in mind. He wished for a wife, a trailer house, a new Chevy, and a job driving semis. Man's needs are simple and his wants are few, but his lusts are strong and of great variety.

CORKY OBERLANDER was born into a German Lutheran family on a cotton farm outside Roscoe, Texas. He graduated from high school and served a hitch in the army engineers. Afterward, he returned home and used his army-learned surveying skills to get a job with the Highway Department in Abilene.

In 1959, Corky married Peggy Sue Roberts from Sweetwater. The marriage lasted only a few short months before she ran off with a core drill operator. (Peggy Sue always was about half-wild.) After the divorce, Corky spent a weekend getting drunk and laid in Juarez, Mexico. Then he stoically went back to work.

Corky likes to fish, hunt, play softball, and drink a few beers. He was having a few beers when he found himself at Red Grover's bar in Bradleyville and met a young lady named Lu Ann Hampton Laverty.

TOWN FOLK

L. D. ALEXANDER grew up in Bradleyville and married his high-school sweetheart. After his return from World War II, L.D. went to work for A.B.C. Supermarkets, Inc. He soon rose to the rank of manager, a modest but respectable position in Bradleyville's middle-class society. L.D. has two children, a boy and a girl. L.D. believes in white supremacy. L.D. is the guy with the green apron and the tag that says MGR. He is usually standing around the checkout stand.

RAMSEY-EYES BLANKENSHIP has lived in Bradleyville since he was ten years old and has known the secondhand existence of a West Texas black. In his own world, he is simply known as Granddaddy; in the white world he is Ramsey-Eyes. His full name, Ramsey Washington Blankenship has been used twice—once when he was baptized and once when he was married. It will not be used again until his funeral. Since the death of his wife, Ramsey-Eyes has lived by himself in a small, sagging, three-room house. Most of his children have moved to bigger cities and his grandchildren upset him with their mutterings about social change. As long as Ramsey-Eyes can earn his keep and go fishing every weekend, then he is content. He moves through his old age like a shuffling shadow.

MILO CRAWFORD was born and raised in Bradleyville. He was five years old when his father died, and Milo, an only child, came under his mother's grip. After graduating from high school, Milo was spared the draft when his mother claimed he was her sole support. For many years now Milo has worked at the Bradleyville Grain and Feed Store. Milo has contemplated marriage now and again, but the thought of leaving Mama is too painful for him to get seriously involved with a bride-to-be. Milo has made two great decisions in his life without consulting Mama: one, to take up cigarette smoking, and the other, to join the Knights of the White Magnolia, both decisions being mild forms of rebellion. To counteract these moves, Mama hides the ashtrays and tries to think up little errands for him to run on meeting nights.

RED GROVER is originally from Meridian, Mississippi. Red came to Bradleyville following its brief oil boom right after World War II, a conflict he served in totally without distinction. When the "homecoming G.I.'s" defeated the Baptists in the local "wet, dry election," Red took his savings and put up Red's Place, a bar and package liquor store. When the boom had run itself out and the wells were capped, Red found himself shunned by most of the townspeople and, like most bar owners, developed a deep disgust for his clients. Never taking a wife, Red rides out his sexual desires on skinny-legged barmaids and drunken divorcees and grows more and more bitter as the days and nights drag on.

RUFE PHELPS as a young man worked in various oil fields around West Texas. However, after he married, he settled down to a more permanent position at the refinery.

OLIN POTTS grew up on a family farm and stayed there. He married late in life and lives out at his place with his wife and mother. Olin and Rufe are both childless and have kept up a competitive struggle that began in grade school. They went through their softball and rodeo stage and are now hard at each other at checkers, fishing, dove hunting, horseshoes, and dominoes. Their ages and occupations kept them out of

World War II and they spent the war years running trotlines and betting on the outcome of battles.

MIKE TREMAINE has lived in Bradleyville all his life. He is married and has three children. Mike grows watermelon and cotton on a small farm outside of town. He also works as general handyman for Floyd Kinkaid and has done so for about a year.

THE KINKAID FAMILY

COLONEL J. C. KINKAID is old and confined to a wheelchair. He was born in 1887 on his father's ranch, and in his youth he enjoyed the soft life that a cattle and cotton empire could provide. In his later years the God of Fortune that looks down on and loves us all added a further bonanza to him in the form of oil wells. He attended high school at Mirabeau B. Lamar Military Academy and went on to Texas A&M, choosing a military career over ranch life. The Colonel served with General John Pershing in the Philippines, in Mexico, and finally in France during World War I. What started out to be a fulfilling military career in the Philippines ended in the trenches in France. "The Colonel returned from the great war to continue in his family's business interests in and around Bradleyville, Texas, and is interested in many civic organizations," or so his paragraph reads in the *Texas Who's Who.* Actually, the Colonel returned from France shattered in mind and body. Luckily for the family, an older brother kept the fortune together until the Colonel's son Floyd took up his father's half of the business and simply let the Colonel ramble on into his lost world of memories. Now in his dotage, the Colonel's string is starting to run out.

FLOYD KINKAID is a power in this small town and he knows it. Floyd's interests are many and his hobbies are expensive: registered quarter horses, a big flashy bass boat, charter membership in the country club. He was twice president of the Jaycees and is a leading figure in all civic organizations. Floyd and his older brother, Franklin, were both born in Bradleyville after the Colonel's return from World War I. They attended Bradleyville High and both graduated from college—Franklin from Texas A&M and Floyd from Texas Tech. When World War II broke out, Franklin went into the air force and Floyd joined the navy. Franklin was killed when his B-17 crashed in Florida, and Floyd wound up attached to a headquarters section in San Diego. After the war, Floyd married Maureen and returned to Bradleyville to take control of his father's business interests. Floyd and his Uncle Brewster Kinkaid have turned the Kinkaid holdings into a sizable money-making venture. Now, with the business virtually running itself, Floyd is becoming bored and is casting about for other interests.

MAUREEN KINKAID was born in Bradleyville of a moderately well-to-do family. She graduated from Bradleyville High and went on to Texas Tech, majoring in secondary education. She and Floyd had dated all through high school and had planned to get married after graduating from college. However, the war changed all that. Floyd went into the navy and Maureen did her bit on the Bradleyville home front answering "V" mail and collecting tinfoil. When the war was over, she and Floyd married and set up housekeeping in town. In 1957 Floyd built the new house and they moved to their present location. They have no children. Floyd secretly blames her and she secretly blames him, but neither has bothered to find out anything for sure. Maureen wonders why she's so goddamned bored with everything.

THE SICKENGER FAMILY

MARTHA ANN SICKENGER is also a Bradleyville girl. Her family owns the grain and feed store. Martha Ann graduated from high school in 1953 and was considered at the time to be "a little bit on the wild side." After a disastrous one semester at Texas University, Martha Ann returned home and grabbed off Clarence Sickenger, much to the town's amusement, Clarence being thirty-four at the time. However, their two children, Howard and Charlotte Marie, came bouncing into being and everybody came around to admitting that it might be a pretty good match after all. Martha Ann seems to think so, and if Clarence just happens to be one of the richest men in town, well, "what the hell."

CLARENCE SICKENGER is also a lifelong Bradleyville citizen; like Floyd, he too comes from a wealthy family. He graduated from Texas University and spent World War II right in Bradleyville—exempt from the draft because of his value to the oil industry. In 1953, Clarence married Martha Ann Montgomery and they settled down to a life of small-town wealth. Although Clarence and Floyd have never been close friends, they started a conversation out at the country-club bar the other day that had the makings of a real partnership.

The Last Meeting
of the Knights of the
White Magnolia

Characters

RAMSEY-EYES BLANKENSHIP *Seventy-five. Black custodian of the Cattleman's Hotel*

RUFE PHELPS *Fifty-five. Refinery worker*

OLIN POTTS *Fifty-six. Cotton farmer*

RED GROVER *Forty-eight. Owner of Red's Place, a small bar*

L. D. ALEXANDER *Forty-nine. Manager of A.B.C. Supermarket*

COLONEL J. C. KINKAID *Seventy-five. Colonel, U.S. Army (Ret.). Owner of Cattleman's Hotel*

SKIP HAMPTON *Thirty-one. Texaco service station attendant*

LONNIE ROY MCNEIL *Twenty-one. Pipe fitter at Silver City Pipe Company*

MILO CRAWFORD *Twenty-six. Clerk at Bradleyville Grain & Feed*

ACT I

The time is 1962 in Bradleyville, Texas. The setting is the meeting room of the Knights of the White Magnolia on the third floor of the Cattleman's Hotel. The plastered walls are stained and faded, the floor warped and splintered, patched here and there with flat tin cans. Chairs of various ages, colors, and styles are scattered about the room. One is an old wheelchair. At one end of the room (stage right) is a small podium on a low platform. On the face of the podium is painted a rather smudged white magnolia flower. On the wall behind the podium are two flags, "The Stars and Bars" and the "Lone Star," both very old and very dirty. Between the two flags hangs a cross made of light bulbs. Stage left is the door into the room. Along the upstage wall is a coat rack. On the floor by the coat rack is an old trunk containing the initiation hats. Hanging on the stage-left and upstage wall are old banners representing the sun, the moon, and the west wind.

As the scene opens, it is early evening. RAMSEY-EYES *is listlessly sweeping the floor. He is an old black man in very old clothes. As he sweeps the floor he hums and sings snatches of "Red River Valley."*

After a bit we hear the voices of RUFE PHELPS *and* OLIN POTTS. RUFE *wears khaki work clothes and a baseball cap.* OLIN *wears Levi's, a cotton work shirt, and a straw hat.*

RUFE

(Offstage.) Ah been playin' horseshoes since Jesus H. Christ was a windmill salesman and ah never seen nuthin' like it.

OLIN

(Offstage.) What the hell are you talkin' about?

RUFE

(Entering.) Ah wouldn't play horseshoes with you again, Olin Potts, if you was the last man left in West Texas, and that's by-God fact.

RAMSEY-EYES

Howdy, Mr. Rufe. Howdy, Mr. Olin.

OLIN

(Entering.) Aw hell, Rufe, ah never done nuthin'.

RUFE

Never done nuthin'! Never done nuthin'! Hell, ah spoze cheatin' is nuthin'. Nuthin' to *you*, that is. No, sir, to a fella like *you*, cheatin' is jest nuthin' atall.

RAMSEY-EYES

How is you-all this evenin'?

OLIN

Now listen here, Rufe Phelps, ah never cheated!

RUFE

Never cheated! Well, ah don't know what cheatin' is if what you done *wasn't*.

RAMSEY-EYES

Shore been hot today, ain't it!?

OLIN

(Sitting.) Ah never cheated.

RUFE
Did it!

OLIN
Didn't!

RAMSEY-EYES
You-all is kinda early tonight, ain't you?

RUFE
That last throw of mine was a leaner.

OLIN
Weren't neither.

RUFE
Was too!

OLIN
Weren't!

RUFE
How's come it weren't?

OLIN
Cause for a leaner to be a leaner, it's gotta by Gawd lean!

RUFE
If that last throw of mine wasn't leanin' ah'd sure as hell like
to know what it was doin'.

OLIN
It was lyin' flat on its butt in the dirt. That's what it was doin'.

RAMSEY-EYES
Yes, sah, horseshoes is a mighty good game, okay.

(The door opens and RED GROVER *appears.* RED *is fat, thick-
necked, and cynical. He wears a rumpled blue suit with a*

*flowered necktie. He carries a paper bag containing four
bottles of cheap bourbon.)*

RUFE
Hey, Red, when is a leaner a leaner?

RED
Who gives a damn!

RAMSEY
Howdy, Mistah Grover, how is you?

OLIN
That last toss of yours weren't no leaner no way.

RUFE
Was by Gawd too.

OLIN
Weren't.

RED
What you two monkey-nuts fightin' about now?

RUFE
My last throw over to the horseshoes was a leaner and Olin
cheated and said it weren't.

OLIN
Well, it weren't.

RUFE
Wouldn't surprise me none if maybe you didn't kick it a little
bit.

OLIN
Ah never kicked nuthin'. There was no way to kick nuthin'
no ways, 'cause that damned horseshoe weren't leanin'.

RUFE
Was so too. You cheated!

OLIN
Didn't done it.

RUFE
Did too.

OLIN
Didn't!

RED
For Christ's sake, if all you two are gonna do is fight about it, why don't you quit playin'?

RUFE
Well, hell, Red, ah like to play.

RED
Play with somebody else then.

OLIN
Ain't nobody else to play with.

RAMSEY-EYES
Well, iffen you-all is gonna start on wif de meetin' here, ah'll jest go on down to de lobby. *(He exits.)*

RED
(Hearing door close.) Who the hell was that?

RUFE
Ramsey-Eyes, ah think.

RED
Well, goddamn, ah guess he's gittin' too uppity to talk to

people any more. Ah swear, it's gittin' nowadays where by God you gotta talk to *them* first.

OLIN
That's about it.

(The door opens and L. D. ALEXANDER *enters.* L.D. *is big and florid. He wears a baggy J. C. Penney Western suit, scuffed black loafers with white socks, and a small white Stetson hat.)*

L.D.
Howdy, brothers.

RUFE
Howdy, L.D.

L.D.
Man, it's dark in here. *(Touches switch. After general greeting)* You bring the re-freshments there, Red?

RED
You bet, L.D. *(He indicates paper bag.)* Best stock ah got in the house.

L.D.
I'll bet. *(He picks a bottle out of the bag.)* Old Buzzard Puke. Yes, sir, Red, this looks like real smooth stuff.

RUFE
Old Buzzard Puke. That's a good one, ain't it, Olin?

OLIN
Shore is.

RED
Ah don't notice you-all passin' any of it up when it comes round.

L.D.
Well, you can bet your butt Skip Hampton won't pass it up.

RED
Hell, Skip wouldn't pass up a drink if he had to squeeze it out of an armadillo's ass.

RUFE
Hey, ah got a good idea. Let's hide the whiskey and play like we ain't got any when Skip comes in.

RED
There ain't any place in this whole world to hide whiskey from Skip. He'd sniff it out if it wuz wrapped in lead.

RUFE
No, no. What we do, you see, is hide these-here bottles and then tell Skip that it was *his* turn to bring the re-freshments. Then he won't know. You see?

OLIN
Hey, that's a good one, Rufe.

RED
Might work at that.

OLIN
(*To* RUFE) How'd you happen to think up a good one like that?

RUFE
Well, hell, Olin, ah think of things sometimes.

(*Offstage, ad lib of* SKIP *and* RAMSEY-EYES.)

OLIN
You ain't never thought of nuthin' affore.

RUFE
Now listen here, Olin Potts . . .

(The door opens and SKIP HAMPTON *enters.* SKIP *is a pale, thin, blond-headed man. He wears a greasy green Texaco uniform.)*

SKIP
Howdy, ever'body.

L.D.
Well, howdy there, Skip, how's the boy?

SKIP
Pretty good.

RUFE
Hey, Skip, didn't you forgit somethin'?

SKIP
No, ah don't think so.

RED
Aw, come on now, Skip. Don't try to kid your old buddies.

SKIP
Ah ain't kiddin' nobody.

RUFE
Old Skip. Always tryin' to kid his buddies.

SKIP
Ah ain't kiddin', ah tell you. What the hell you-all talkin' about?

RED
What are we talkin' about? Well, hell's fire, boy, we're talking about the re-freshments.

SKIP
What about the re-freshments?

L.D.
Where the hell are they?

SKIP
Ah don't know where they are.

RED
You mean to say you didn't bring them?

SKIP
Me? No, ah didn't bring nuthin'.

L.D.
Well, Gawd Almighty damn!

RUFE
Now we ain't got nuthin' to drink.

SKIP
Red always brings them samples from the package store, he always does.

RED
Now, Skip. You know ah told you to pick it up for me and bring it over here for tonight's meetin'.

RUFE
Shore he did. He told you to, Skip. Didn't he, Olin?

OLIN
Shore did.

SKIP
No, you didn't, Red. Ah swear to God you never. Ah would of remembered. Hell's fire, ah'd never forget somethin' as important as that.

L.D.
Well, looks like we jest gotta do without tonight.

SKIP
No, wait. Ah'll go back and git it, Red. Ah'll jest run over to your place and pick some up!

RED
Too late now. Ah done locked up the package store.

SKIP
Well, you can open it again, can't you? Give me the key, ah'll go.

RED
You? Give *you* the key to mah hard liquor. You gotta be crazy, boy, that would be like givin' old L.D. here a Charg-a-Plate to a whorehouse.

SKIP
Well, let somebody else go then. How about Rufe here?

RUFE
Why should ah go do what you was supposed to do but forgot? *(He and* OLIN *both giggle.)*

SKIP
(Truth suddenly dawning on him) Whatta you guys tryin' to pull?

L.D.
Well, hell, since old Skip let us down tonight, ah guess we gotta make do with this. *(He pulls out the sack.)*

RUFE
Gotcha there, Skip. We really gotcha there.

SKIP
(Dully) Yeah, boy, that was a good one, okay.

OLIN
Rufe thought it up.

SKIP
(Sarcastically) Damn good goin' there, Rufe. *(He reaches for the sack.)*

RED
(Stopping him.) Now hold on there. All us *gentlemen* wait on refreshments till after the meetin', don't we, Skip?

SKIP
Sure, sure, oh, hell, yes.

(The door opens and RAMSEY-EYES *pokes his head in.)*

RAMSEY-EYES
'Scuse me.

RED
What the hell you want, Ramsey-Eyes?

RAMSEY
Ah jest come up to say how Floyd done brought his daddy to the meetin'. He's down in de lobby now.

L.D.
Okay, Ramsey-Eyes. *(The door closes.)* Rufe, you and Olin go on down and git Colonel Kinkaid.

RUFE
Okay, L.D.

(They start to exit.)

L.D.
And be careful with him comin' up the stairs.

OLIN
We ain't never dropped him yet.

L.D.
Old Colonel Kinkaid, by God, he's somethin' else, ain't he?
Here he is all crippled up and almost blind, but wild horses
wouldn't keep him from a lodge meeting. No, sir.

SKIP
How old is the Colonel nowadays, L.D.?

L.D.
Well, let's see, ah reckin he must be at least seventy-five.

SKIP
No kiddin'.

L.D.
You bet; hell, all them Kinkaids is tough. All except Floyd,
that is.

RED
Oh, that old man ain't so tough.

L.D.
Hell he ain't.

RED
Well, goddamn, L.D., he's got the shell shocks, ain't he? All
you gotta do is belch too loud and he starts yellin' about the
Germans coming after him.

L.D.
Hell, Red, there were lots of fellers come back from
that World's War I with the shell shocks, and even with them
he's still more of a man than that damn Floyd will ever
be.

SKIP

That's the damn truth. You know, it's kind of funny what with Floyd and that gnat-titted wife of his, what's her name?

L.D.

Maureen.

SKIP

Maureen, bein' the high by-God so-ciety in this-here town, why ain't Floyd ever joined our lodge?

RED

'Cause he thinks it's a bunch of bullshit, that's why. All Floyd and old gnat-tits and the rest of the rich bastards in this town wanna do is sit around the goddamned country club and play kneesies. Floyd lets the Colonel come up here to the meetings so's everyone can see how nice he is to his daddy. But you watch, the minute the Colonel kicks off, Floyd's gonna close this-here hotel before the carcass is cold.

L.D.

Oh no, now he wouldn't do a thing like that.

RED

The hell he wouldn't. Floyd may be a bastard, but he's not a stupid bastard. You see how many payin' guests are in this-here fire trap? Probably about five. This mighta been a classy hotel way back yonder when the Colonel had it built, but that Holiday Inn out to the bypass done kicked this dump plumb outta business.

L.D.

That don't mean a goddamn thing. Nobody's gonna close down this place. Hell, Red, this-here Cattleman's Hotel is a by-God landmark in this country.

RED

Oh, hell yes, the whole town of Bradleyville is a by-God landmark, but that didn't stop the state from runnin' the highway around it. Take a look down Main Street for Christ's sake, there's so many damned stores bein' boarded up that the only outfit in town that's makin' any money is the god-damned used-lumber company.

L.D.

Well, ah admit that things is kindly slow but . . .

RED

Oh, you admit that, do you? *(He starts to laugh.)*

L.D.

What the hell's so funny?

RED

I just happened to think, what if Floyd don't close the place down but turns it into a hotel for Coloreds only? By God, that would damn sure play hell with the old meetin' night.

*(*L.D. *and* SKIP *stare at him.)*

L.D.

Well, what the hell!

RED

Oh, I'm jest kiddin', of course. Floyd would never do nuthin' like that.

L.D.

He damn sure wouldn't.

RED

(Still amused) 'Course he wouldn't.

(Offstage dialogue before COLONEL*'s entrance.)*

COLONEL
(Offstage) Watch what you're doin', damnit, you're not totin'
a bale of alfalfa!

RUFE
(Offstage) Ah'm sorry, Colonel. Confound it, Olin, hold up
your part!

OLIN
(Offstage) Ah am holdin' up my part. You're the one not
doin' nuthin'.

RUFE
(Offstage) Now listen here, Olin Potts.

COLONEL
(Offstage) Shut the hell up, the both of you. Now open that
damn door, Ramsey-Eyes.

RAMSEY-EYES
Yes sah, Colonel. *(He opens the door and goes to the wheelchair to arrange it.*

*(OLIN and RUFE carry in the COLONEL. The COLONEL is
dressed in gabardine Western pants, slippers, and a faded,
patched World War I officer's tunic. His legs are crippled and
he is nearly blind.)*

RAMSEY-EYES
Ah got you chair here, Colonel Kinkaid, sah.

COLONEL
Good man, Ramsey-Eyes.

*(OLIN and RUFE start to ease the COLONEL into the wheel-
chair.)*

OLIN
Damnit, Rufe, be careful with his legs.

RUFE
Damnit yourself, ah know what ah'm doin'.

COLONEL
(Settling into wheelchair.) All right, all right, ah'm in, now git away from me, the both of you!

RUFE
Boy howdy, them steps up from the lobby is gittin' hard to climb.

RAMSEY-EYES
(Arranging COLONEL*'s lap robe.)* Ah'll be right down in the lobby iffen you need anythin'.

COLONEL
Right, Ramsey-Eyes, DISMISSED. *(*RAMSEY-EYES *doesn't move.)* What the hell you waitin' for?

RAMSEY-EYES
Is you wearin' your dentures tonight, Colonel?

COLONEL
Hell yes, ah'm wearin' my teeth. *(Points to them.)* See.

RAMSEY-EYES
You know what Floyd said 'bout wearin' your dentures.

COLONEL
Ah know what he said; now, damnit, *dismissed!*

RAMSEY-EYES
(Exiting.) Yes, sah, but Floyd said you gotta wear your dentures.

L.D.
Howdy, Colonel Kinkaid.

COLONEL
Howdy, boys. How you-all tonight?

SKIP
Howdy, Colonel.

COLONEL
Who is it?

SKIP
Skip Hampton, Colonel.

COLONEL
Well, howdy there, Skip. How's your sister?

SKIP
She's jest fine, Colonel.

COLONEL
And your mother?

SKIP
Couldn't be better.

COLONEL
Ah used to court your Aunt Sally. Betcha didn't know that,
did you?

SKIP
Yeah, Colonel, you told me.

COLONEL
Slapped mah face so hard one night it knocked me plumb
outta the buckboard.

L.D.
Sure, Colonel.

COLONEL

Thought for a second that damned buggy whip ah had in mah hand was a lightnin' rod.

L.D.

(Going behind podium.) Well, we might as well git started.

RUFE

Where's old Milo Crawford tonight?

L.D.

Milo can't make it. He phoned over to the house and said he hadda take his mama over to Big Spring.

RED

Jesus Christ—wouldn't you know it.

L.D.

(Banging on podium with his hand.) Okay now. This-here meetin' of the Bradleyville, Texas, Lodge of the Knights of the White Magnolia is now in order. Ever'body 'cept the Colonel stand up and repeat the oath.

ALL

(In a rather ragged cadence) "Ah swear as a true Knight of the White Magnolia to preserve the merits handed to me by mah forefathers and to hold as a sacred trust the ideals of mah Southern heritage. Ah pledge mah life to the principles of White Magnolia-ism and will obey until ah die the laws of this-here so-ciety."

L.D.

Okay, ever'body can sit down now. (OLIN *starts to the door.)* Where the hell you goin', Olin?

OLIN

(Surprised) Ah'm goin' on out to git the card tables so's we can commence with the domino games.

L.D.
Well, you can jest sit on back down, 'cause we ain't havin' no dominoes tonight.

OLIN
No dominoes? What kinda meetin' can we have with no dominoes?

COLONEL
Damnit, ah wanna shuffle dominoes!

L.D.
We ain't playin' no dominoes tonight, Colonel.

COLONEL
Why not?

L.D.
'Cause tonight we're gonna have us a real meetin'!

RED
What the hell you talkin' about?

L.D.
Tonight we're gonna have us a real live initiation.

SKIP
You mean to tell us that somebody wants to join the lodge?

L.D.
That's right.

RED
Well, ah'll be damned.

L.D.
Brother Knight Rufe Phelps here has got us a new man, ain't you, Brother Knight Phelps?

RUFE
(Grinning and shuffling.) Yes, sir, ah have.

OLIN
You never told me 'bout no new man whilst we was a-playin' horseshoes.

RUFE
Ah was gonna, till you started cheatin'.

OLIN
Ah never cheated! You're the one that cheats. Any time you throw one four feet from the stake you call it a dadburned leaner!

L.D.
All right now, damnit, let's git on with it! Brother Knight Phelps, tell us 'bout our new brother-to-be.

RUFE
Ah got us Lonnie Roy McNeil. He's old Grady McNeil's boy from over there in Silver City . . .

COLONEL
Silver City! Ah won't have him!

RUFE
(Taken aback) He's a real nice feller, Colonel.

COLONEL
Don't give a damn; if he's from Silver City he's no damn good!

SKIP
Well, hell, Colonel, it's not like he's from the Congo or somethin'. My God, Silver City's only three miles away.

L.D.

Ah think it's a right good idea that we branch out a little, Colonel. Ah mean, nobody from Bradleyville has joined the lodge for over five years now.

COLONEL

People from Silver City are low-down stinkin' cowards and ah flat will not have them around!

RUFE

Well, hell, ah didn't know *Silver City* was on our list too!

L.D.

Now, Colonel, you know we all respect your judgment in ever'thang but . . .

COLONEL

You damn well better.

L.D.

But maybe we would all understand a little better if we all knew *why* people from Silver City was no damn good.

COLONEL

Because in nineteen hundred and eighteen Staff Sergeant George Plummer from right over yonder in Silver City refused to fight, that's why! Whey-faced little coward jest stood there in the trench with his puttees floppin' around and puke all over his face, hands shakin' and spit runnin' out his mouth. Kept mumblin' over and over, "Who am ah? Who am ah?" Well, ah knew damn well who he was, he was Staff Sergeant George Plummer from over there to *Silver City*. Ah ordered that little son-of-a-bitch to climb up . . . people from Silver City are no damn good. That is an order and that is a fact.

L.D.

Well, hell, Colonel, this-here feller wantin' to join ain't no Plummer, he's a McNeil.

RUFE
That's right, Colonel, he's old Grady McNeil's boy.

COLONEL
He's from *Silver City,* ain't he?

RUFE
Well, yes, but . . .

COLONEL
Well, there you are.

L.D.
Well, actually, he ain't exactly from Silver City, Colonel. Ah mean, not from right there smack in the town. The McNeil place is sorter outside the town, isn't it, Rufe?

RUFE
Well, yeah, kindly out on the rural route there.

COLONEL
Not in the town, huh?

RUFE
No, sir. Now, Lonnie Roy works there in Silver City but he lives sorter out, you know.

COLONEL
Well, ah don't know. You're sure now he's not a Plummer?

RUFE
Oh no, sir, Colonel, he's a McNeil, okay and he's shore wantin' to be a Lodge brother. Ah talked to him day affore yesterday over to the Silver City Pipe Fittin' Company and he said he would come over here tonight for shore.

COLONEL
Which McNeil is that?

L.D.

Grady McNeil's boy, Colonel. From over there to Silver, uh, uh, from over yonder.

COLONEL

That the Grady McNeil that married the oldest Richey girl?

RUFE

No, ah think Lonnie Roy's Mama was a Spencer, weren't she, Olin?

OLIN

(Who is an expert in these matters, therefore he pronounces each name very distinctly.) She was *Maude Spencer* affore she married *Grady McNeil* over there to, uh, *by* Silver City. I know this 'cause a bunch of my cousins is *Spencers* and *Maude* was the second-oldest girl next to *Winifred Spencer,* who married a P & G soap salesman from Amarillo.

RUFE

By God, that's right. I remember that. Married him kindly on the sly, didn't she?

OLIN

They e-loped up to Durant, Oklahoma. Made her pa mad as hell. He didn't want *Winifred* married to no drummer. Ah remember 'cause her brother *Clete* an' me was pullin' a water well once out to the *Honeycutt* place and . . .

RED

For Christ's sake, let's git on with the meetin'!

OLIN

Ah jest thought you-all wanted to know.

RED

Well, we don't. Come on, L.D., let's git on with it.

L.D.

Yes, well, it sounds like Lonnie Roy's got himself a real fine background, Brother Knight Potts.

OLIN

(Smugly) Figgered you-all wanted to know.

RUFE

That the same Clete Spencer that drowned out to Lake Bradleyville?

SKIP

For Christ's sake!

OLIN

No, if you recall, there was two *Clete Spencers*. You see *Winifred*'s daddy married twice. Now the *Clete Spencer* ah was pullin' the well with was known as *"Big Clete"* *Spencer* 'cause he was borned to *old man Spencer's* first wife, *Bessie*, who was also the mama of *Winifred* and *Maude*, but the other *Clete Spencer*, who was knowed as *"Little Clete"* and who drowned out to Lake Bradleyville, was borned to *old man Spencer's* second wife, *Mary*, who was also the mama of . . .

SKIP

Jesus Christ. Sure, Olin, we all know the story. Now come on, let's git on with the meetin'.

RUFE

You don't want to git on with the meetin'. You jest want to git on with the refreshments.

SKIP

Ah do not!

RED

The hell you don't. Your tongue's hangin' out so far now it looks like a necktie.

COLONEL

Onward, onward. Quit dilly-dallying around. Git the job done. The A.E.F. never wasted time. Never would have whipped the Hun if we had. Git the job done.

L.D.

Yes, sir, Colonel. Now, as ah was sayin . . . *(He is interrupted by a commotion outside the door. Shouts and bangs.)*

OLIN

(Leaping up.) Oh, my God, what's that?

(The door bursts open and RAMSEY-EYES *appears, securely holding on to a young man—*LONNIE ROY MCNEIL.*)*

RAMSEY-EYES

Ah got him! Ah got him! He was tryin' to sneak into the meetin', Mistah L.D., sah, but ah glommed onto him affore he could.

LONNIE

Tell this crazy fool to turn me loose!

RUFE

Let him go, Ramsey-Eyes, this here is Lonnie Roy McNeil.

RAMSEY-EYES

(Releasing him.) You mean he belongs up here?

RED

That's right, *he* belongs up here, but *you* don't. Now git your butt back down to the lobby where it does belong.

RAMSEY-EYES

Yes, sah, ah only wishes you-all would tell me who am a Magnolia and who ain't, thass all. *(Exits.)*

COLONEL

What happened, what's goin' on?

L.D.

Nuthin', Colonel Kinkaid. Jest a little misunderstandin', that's all.

SKIP

Ramsey-Eyes jest made a little mistake, Colonel, that's all.

COLONEL

Ramsey-Eyes. He a member now?

L.D.

'Course he ain't no member, Colonel, he jest caught some-body outside, thinkin' it was an in-truder.

COL.

Caught him a spy, did he? Good man, that Ramsey-Eyes. Good soldier.

RUFE

Only it weren't no spy. It was Lonnie Roy McNeil, our new member.

RED

Stupid black, dumb butt!

(They all turn and contemplate LONNIE ROY. *He is a thin, big-eyed kid in an ill-fitting suit; his hair is bowl cut and he wears tennis shoes. Born on a little farm just outside Silver City, Texas,* LONNIE ROY *had watched his older brothers march off to Korea and envisioned a military ca-reer for himself. However, physical defects, asthma, and flat feet kept him out of service. He left high school in his sophomore year and was employed by a pipe-fitting con-cern. For a while he enjoyed the company of his fellow dropouts and high-school chums—driving around in pickup trucks, smoking cigarettes, and drinking beer—but soon the long arm of the draft board and in one or two cases, the state penitentiary in Huntsville cut his peer*

group down to one. LONNIE ROY *found himself enjoying the comradeship of absolutely no one at all until one day* RUFE PHELPS *dropped into Silver City to buy some pipe.)*

L.D.
Howdy there, Lonnie Roy. Mah name is L. D. Alexander and ah wish to welcome you to the Knights of the White Magnolia.

LONNIE   .
Jeeezus, that's one mean man you got out there.

L.D.
Ah hell, boy, Ramsey-Eyes ain't one of us. He jest sweeps up the place, that's all.

LONNIE
Oh well, ah guess that's all right then. You sure now he ain't . . .

L.D.
Hell no! Now come on and meet the fellow knights. This here is Red Grover.

RED
How are you?

L.D.
Rufe Phelps you already know. *(They nod.)* Olin Potts over by the door there.

OLIN
Your mama is *Maude Spencer McNeil,* ain't she?

LONNIE
Yes, sir, she is.

OLIN
Knew it!

L.D.
Skip Hampton.

SKIP
Howdy.

L.D.
And Colonel J. C. Kinkaid.

COLONEL
Retired. Glad to know you, Lonnie Roy. What branch you serve in?

LONNIE
Beg pardon.

COLONEL
Army, Navy, Marines, Army Air Corps?

LONNIE
Oh, that. Nuthin'.

COLONEL
Nuthin'?

LONNIE
I git the asthma sometimes.

COLONEL
Well, what the hell.

LONNIE
(Lifting a tennis-shoe-clad foot.) An mah feet is flat.

COLONEL
Jesus Christ!

LONNIE
Well, gawlee, ah cain't help it.

L.D.
The Colonel here was in the A.E.F.

LONNIE
The what?

L.D.
The American Army in World's War I.

LONNIE
Ah don't reckon ah ever studied much on them ancient wars and such like.

COLONEL
Blackball the flat-footed asthmatic, *Silver City* son-of-a-bitch!

LONNIE
Hell, ah never meant nuthin'.

L.D.
'Course you didn't, Lonnie Roy. The Colonel here is jest a little crusty, that's all. He don't mean no harm.

RED
Jest an old war horse, right, Colonel?

COLONEL
Better an old war horse than a young jackass!

L.D.
Now, you jest sit down right here, Lonnie Roy, and we'll git on with the meetin'. Then afterwards we'll all have us a little nip. How's that sound?

SKIP
Sounds damn good to me.

L.D.
Shut up, Skip.

LONNIE
Fine, fine. A little nip would go down real good.

SKIP
Sure would!

RED
Shut up, Skip!

L.D.
Now, Lonnie Roy, affore ah ad-minister the oath of member-
ship, ah want to tell you a little bit about the Knights of the
White Magnolia.

LONNIE
Rufe already told me about the domino games. Sounds real
good to me.

RUFE
Old Lonnie Roy here really likes them dominoes.

LONNIE
You bet! Moon, Forty-two, ah like to play 'em all.

OLIN
We play mostly Forty-two here, Lonnie Roy.

LONNIE
And when he told me that this-here lodge was for white
men only, well, sir, ah was sold. Sold right there on the
spot.

L.D.
That's fine, Lonnie Roy, but now let me tell you about the
rest . . .

LONNIE

When Rufe come over to the pipe-fittin' company and told me about this-here lodge, ah said right off, "Sign me up," didn't ah, Rufe?

RUFE

Shore did. Ah was over there buyin' some pipe for mah cesspool . . .

LONNIE

You can git it over yonder a whole lot cheaper than here in Bradleyville.

RUFE

That's the damn truth.

L.D.

Well, that's fine, now . . .

OLIN

What you gittin' for pipe over there, Lonnie Roy?

L.D.

Damnit to hell, now you all shut up and let me finish.

OLIN

Well, all ah wanted to know was . . .

RED

Shut up, Olin!

COLONEL

What's happenin'? What's goin' on?

SKIP

Red won't let L.D. git on with the meetin'.

RED

The hell you say! Ah never done nuthin'. It was Olin.

OLIN
Ah never done nuthin'.

COLONEL
Shut the hell up, all of you! Now damnit, L.D., git on with the meetin'. By gawd, ah wish ah'd had the bunch of you over there in France. You'd have shaped up then, by Gawd.

L.D.
Yes, sir, Colonel . . . now . . .

COLONEL
You'd have shaped up or ah'da kicked some butts!

L.D.
Yes, sir, Colonel.

COLONEL
No goddamned gabbin' around in the trenches. Find yourself strung out on the wire like a piece of pork. Piece of pork.

L.D.
Please, Colonel. If ah can continue.

COLONEL
Yes, yes, continue. Who the hell's stoppin' you?

L.D.
Nobody, Colonel, it's jest that . . .

COLONEL
You let me know who's stoppin' you, L.D., and ah'll put him up again' the by-God wall.

SKIP
Goddamnit, Colonel Kinkaid, shut up!

(There is a long, stunned silence. All turn and look at SKIP.*)*

COLONEL

Who said that! *(Silence.)* Who said that, ah said!!!

SKIP

(Meekly) Ah did, Colonel.

COLONEL

You know the last person who ever dared say that to me?

SKIP

No, sir.

COLONEL

(Animated and cheery) General Pershing, that's who. Old Black Jack himself. *(Chuckles.)* We was down in Mexico at the time and ah was a snotnosed shavetail. Well, sir, one afternoon at the officers' mess . . .

L.D.

Please, Colonel, let's save the story till refreshment time, okay?

RED

Shore, Colonel, let's hold her off till then.

COLONEL

Sure, sure, sure. *(Chuckles.)* Old Black Jack himself.

L.D.

Now, Lonnie Roy, as ah was sayin', bein' a member of the Knights of the White Magnolia is actual bein' a member of a brotherhood. Ah mean, you can look on any of us fellers here just like we was your own brothers, your own blood kin.

LONNIE

(Sincerely) That there's real nice to know.

L.D.

The Knights of the White Magnolia was founded back in 1902,

when Knight Brother Maynard C. Stempco of Austin got fed up to his ears with the way the Ku Klux was runnin' things and broke off to form his own outfit. Well, sir, the idea growed and growed and by the late 1920's there was Knights of the White Magnolia lodges all over Texas and parts of Oklahoma.

LONNIE
My gosh. How's come Mr. Stempco got fed up with the Klan?

RED
'Cause anybody that's got to put on a white bedsheet to kick a coon's ass has got to be a damn fool, that's why!

LONNIE
Oh, yeah, sure, I see.

L.D.
Why in 1939 we had us a con-vention in Tulsa, Oklahoma, that was attended by two thousand people.

RUFE
The Colonel was there. Weren't you, Colonel?

COLONEL
Got drunk and threw up all over my wheelchair. Made the wheels sticky.

LONNIE
You still have them con-ventions?

L.D.
Well, uh, no, not in a long time, but we're workin' on it, ain't we, Red?

RED
(*Amused*) Oh hell, yes.

LONNIE
Well, how's come you don't have 'em regular?

L.D.
Stupidity, Lonnie Roy. Pure by-God dumb stupidity. People got to where they didn't want to join up any more. Can you imagine that? They didn't want to be Knights of the White Magnolia. They wanted to be Jaycees or Toast Masters or Elks or Lions or Moose, they wanted to be by-God animals, that's right, animals, but not knights. They turned around and stabbed their granddaddies square in the back. Turned up their noses on their race, started kowtowin' to all them-there mi-norities, and little by little the lodges jest sorter dried up. Nobody wanted to join. No new people. Jesus, but we was big once, Lonnie Roy. Hell, there was governors and senators that was Brother Knights. We had con-ventions and barbecues and parades. Took over a whole hotel there in Tulsa. Gawd, and it musta been somethin' to see. Bands playin' and baton girls a-marchin' along. The Grand Imperial Wizard of the brotherhood rode in a big open carriage pulled by six white horses, and up above the whole shebang was this great old big blimp towin' this-here banner sayin' TULSA WELCOMES THE KNIGHTS OF THE WHITE MAGNOLIA. Gawda mighty, now wasn't that somethin'!

LONNIE
Jeeezus, you mean to say that with all that great stuff, that people quit joinin' up?

L.D.
That's right, Lonnie Roy.

LONNIE
My God, why?

L.D.
Ah don't know, Lonnie Roy, ah honestly don't know. When Red an' me come into the lodge after World's War II, why

there musta been fifteen or twenty members. Then fellers jest started a-droppin' out—quit comin'. Oh, ever' now and then somebody would join up, like Skip here, he joined up after Ko-rea.

LONNIE
You was in Ko-rea?

SKIP
Damn right. Blastin' them gooks. Ah was hell on wheels with a B.A.R. Regular John Wayne. Right, Red?

RED
That's what you keep tellin' ever'body.

SKIP
Ah'll never forget the time me an' Dale Laverty was bringin' them Marines down from that-there Chosan reservoir.

RED
For Christ's sake, shut up! We heard that damn story a hundred times.

SKIP
(To LONNIE*)* Ah'll tell you all about it after the meetin', okay?

LONNIE
Swell.

SKIP
It's a hell of a good story.

RUFE
Me and Olin have been members since nineteen and forty-eight, ain't we, Olin?

OLIN
January 24th, 1948. Damn right.

LONNIE
You mean, you fellers is all the members there is?

RUFE
Well, there's Milo Crawford, but he had to take his mama over to Big Spring.

RED
Him and his damn mama. Makes you puke.

LONNIE
What about all the lodges in the other towns?

L.D.
There ain't any more.

LONNIE
You mean they're all gone?

L.D.
Ever' one of em.

RED
We're what you might call the last of the Mo-hicans, boy.

LONNIE
But how can you-all keep this-here room for your meetin's, don't it cost a lot of money?

L.D.
Nope. You see the Colonel there owns the hotel.

LONNIE
Oh, ah see.

RED
Don't pay no dues to this club, boy. Jest lots of fun and lots of whiskey.

L.D.
But the most important thing is the fact that you're wantin'
to join up.

LONNIE
Me? Ah'm important?

L.D.
Shore you are. You see, you can git other smart young fellers
like yourself interested in the lodge.

RUFE
Damn right. You may be the start of a whole new movement,
boy.

LONNIE
Well, ah don't know many fellers mah age over to home.
Most of 'em are either gone off somewhere or are in the
army.

L.D.
But you are a start, don't you see? Yes, sir, a start. Hell, we
may be beginnin' a whole new ball game here.

LONNIE
Ah could maybe talk to some of the fellers at the pipe company.

L.D.
There you go!

LONNIE
(Getting excited.) And mah daddy knows lots and lots of
folks.

L.D.
Damn right! Now you're talkin', boy!

RUFE

By gollies, L.D., maybe we got somethin' here. Maybe we can catch on again.

L.D.

Shore we can. Anythin' can happen. Hell's fire, stuff like this has happened affore. Outfits git kindly down like and jest one little thang gits 'em goin' again, and wham, next thang you know they're back on the top. Bigger and better than affore.

OLIN

You mean big like we was in nineteen and thirty-nine?

L.D.

Sure, why not? Bigger!

SKIP

Oh, for Christ's sake!!!

L.D.

What the hell's wrong with you?

SKIP

You guys are crazy. Jesus Christ, we git one new member in five years and ten minutes later we're bigger than the by-God Woodman of the World.

OLIN

It don't do no harm to plan.

SKIP

Plan! This ain't no plan, it's a dream—a damn-fool dream.

L.D.

You tryin' to say we're damn fools!

SKIP

No, no, ah ain't sayin that. It's only . . .

RED

Only what? If you don't like bein' a member of this goddamn brotherhood, why the hell don't you say so?

SKIP

Ah didn't say that, all ah said was . . .

COLONEL

What's goin' on?

RUFE

Skip Hampton says he don't want to be a knight no more.

SKIP

No, ah never. All ah said was . . .

COLONEL

Shoot the goddamned desertin' son-of-a-bitch!

SKIP

Ah ain't desertin'! All ah said was . . .

COLONEL

Shoot 'em! By God, we shot 'em in France. No reason why we can't shoot 'em right here in Bradleyville.

OLIN

Actual, Skip can't help bein' the way he is, what with his grandmother on his daddy's side bein' a *Bentley.*

COLONEL

A Bentley!

SKIP

Oh, my God!

OLIN

All them Bentleys was mean. Now ah don't want to give no

disrespect to your kinfolk there, Skip, but if you'll look back a bit you'll see jest how mean them *Bentleys* was.

SKIP

Who gives a damn!

OLIN

You ought to! Ah mean, if ah had *Bentley* blood in me, ah damn shore would give a damn.

SKIP

Well, ah don't!

OLIN

Well, you ought to!

RUFE

You better listen to Olin there, Skip. When it comes to kinfolk, old Olin there knows what he's talkin' about.

SKIP

Well, why the hell don't we talk about somethin' else! Jesus, ah'm sick and tired of listenin' to whose Uncle Abraham is married to which Cousin Clarabelle's cross-eyed stepsister.

RUFE

You're jest jealous 'cause Olin here can remember all them names and you cain't remember nuthin'.

SKIP

So he can remember names. So damn what! Let's make him the by-God county clerk and fire the bookkeeper. He can sit on his butt and babble Abernathy to Zackafoozass all day long.

OLIN

Well, now that ain't a very nice thang to say.

RED

Yeah, Skip, why the hell don't you shut up.

SKIP

Shut up, yourself, damnit! Where the hell you git off tellin' people to shut up!

RED

You'd better watch your step there, sonny boy!

L.D.

Now, now, Brothers, let's jest all stand back and cool off a spell. Remember, we got us a new member here. We don't want him to git no wrong ideas about us now, do we?

COLONEL

Shoot him!

LONNIE

My gosh. Do you fellers fight like this all the time?

RED

Only on meetin' nights.

LONNIE

Maybe ah'd better go home and come back next time.

L.D.

No need of that. We're jest horsin' around, that's all. Havin' lots of fun is part of bein' a brother. Why, the best part of the meetin' is comin up, the initiation, and after that the refreshments. You don't wanna miss that, do you?

LONNIE

No, ah jest thought . . .

L.D.

Well, hell no, you don't! We gotta initiation for you, Lonnie

Roy McNeil, that's gonna be the high by-God point of your life.

LONNIE

You ain't gonna hit me with paddles and such like, are you?

L.D.

Hell no! That there's kid stuff, this-here initiation is based on God and brotherhood.

RUFE

It's a hell of an impressive sight, Lonnie Roy—you see, we light up the cross and . . .

OLIN

No fair tellin'! We ain't started yet.

RUFE

Well, hell, ah didn't *tell* nuthin', all ah said was . . .

COLONEL

Let's git on with it! Good God, you men shilly-shally and fart around worse than the Fifth Marines!

SKIP

Hell yes, let's git started!

L.D.

All right, damnit, we will!

COLONEL

Bumble-dickin' around. That's all you fellers do.

L.D.

Yes, well, all right, Colonel. We will now commence with the ceremony of initiation.

OLIN
Wait a minute. We can't start no ceremony yet.

L.D.
Why the hell not?

OLIN
'Cause we ain't voted on him yet.

SKIP
Oh, for Christ's sake.

OLIN
We gotta vote! Them there's the rules.

SKIP
We didn't have no goddamn vote when I got initiated.

RED
It's a damn-good thing for you that we didn't.

SKIP
What the hell's that spozed to mean?

RED
Jest what I said, that's what.

L.D.
All right now, that's jest a by-God nuff! Ah want it quiet in here and ah mean dead quiet. *(Silence.)* That's a whole lot better. All right now, Olin, if you insist, we will . . .

COLONEL
Bumble-dick, bumble-dick, bumble-dick.

L.D.
(Patiently) Yes, Colonel, that's right. Now . . .

COLONEL

That's what old Black Jack did. Bumble-dicked all over Mexico. Let that fat little greaser Pancho Villa make a damn fool of him. Betcha didn't know that, did you?

L.D.

No, Colonel, we didn't. Now . . .

COLONEL

Well, he did.

L.D.

Please, Colonel, we gotta git on with the vote.

COLONEL

What we votin' on?

L.D.

On Lonnie Roy, Colonel.

COLONEL

Who?

L.D.

Lonnie Roy McNeil, our new member.

COLONEL

We got a new member? Well, it's about time; who is it?

RUFE

Lonnie Roy McNeil, Colonel, Grady McNeil's boy from over there to Silver . . . from over yonder.

COLONEL

Well, ah'll be damned. You don't bumble-dick around, do you, young feller?

LONNIE

No, sir!

COLONEL
That's good. The Germans will get you if you do.

LONNIE
(With deep conviction) Well, ah never do.

COLONEL
Come over the top and stick one of them spiky helmets right up your butt.

SKIP
Jesus H. God Almighty, that's the damnedest thang ah ever heard of in my life.

COLONEL
What the hell's wrong with you?

SKIP
Them Germans ain't wore no spiky helmets in fifty years.

COLONEL
Don't mean they ain't gonna put them on again! You-all think the Kaiser's dead, don't you? Well, he ain't! Him and Crown Prince Willie is both livin' on a cattle ranch in Argentina and in secret is storin' up guns in the basements of Catholic churches all over the world.

SKIP
That ain't no Kaiser that's down there in Argentina. That there's *Hitler!* Hell, we've had a whole new world's war since the damn Kaiser was runnin' around.

LONNIE
That's right. Ah remember readin' about old Hitler in school. Why, he was on the German side in World's War II.

RUFE
Only he ain't down in Argentina, no, sir. Ah read in a maga-

zine over to Billberry's Drugstore how them Russians got old
Hitler hid out in a little room over there in Mos-cow.

LONNIE
No kiddin'.

RUFE
Sure. They smuggled him out of Berlin in a hay wagon.

COLONEL
Skinny little son-of-a-bitch couldn't hold a candle to the
Kaiser.

RED
Good God! We gonna git on with the votin' or not?

L.D.
Damn right! Now, everybody in this-here membership wantin' Lonnie Roy McNeil to be a brother knight, put up their
hand.

OLIN
Hold it.

L.D.
Now what?

OLIN
Lonnie Roy here has got to be out of the room when we make
this-here vote. That there's a rule. Ain't it, Rufe?

RUFE
Ah recollect on how it is.

L.D.
Oh, what the hell. Lonnie Roy, would you please leave the
room while we have our vote here.

LONNIE
Shore.

L.D.
Won't take a second. We'll be callin' you right back.

LONNIE
(Moving toward the door.) That's okay, ah'll jest wait outside.

RUFE
Nuthin' to worry about, Lonnie Roy. We jest gotta follow the rules, you know.

LONNIE
Sure, that's okay.

OLIN
Rules is rules.

LONNIE
Fine. *(He exits.)*

L.D.
Okay now, ever'body sit down and we'll com-mence with the votin'. Not you, Olin!

OLIN
How come not me?

L.D.
'Cause you are the door guard tonight.

OLIN
The door guard?

L.D.
You gotta stand up there and guard the door while we have our vote and initiation so's nobody that ain't a Magnolia will slip in on us durin' the ceremony.

OLIN
Well, ah don't wanna stand up all the time.

L.D.
Well, you gotta.

OLIN
Why cain't I sit down and put my foot up again' the door?

L.D.
'Cause you cain't, that's why.

COLONEL
You are the sentry, Olin, and sentries don't sit, they stand and they stand tall.

OLIN
(Grumbling) Yes, sir.

RED
(Chuckling) Rules is rules, Olin.

OLIN
(Mimicking RED's *voice)* Rules is rules, Olin.

L.D.
We will now have our vote.

COLONEL
What we votin' on?

L.D.
On Lonnie Roy, Colonel.

COLONEL
Am ah for him or agin him?

L.D.
You're for him, Colonel.

COLONEL
Hell, ah thought ah was agin him.

(There is another loud commotion outside and MILO CRAW-
FORD *bursts through the door with* LONNIE ROY *in tow.* MILO
*is mild-mannered, lank, gangly, and very homely. He wears
a white shirt, a dark necktie, and an old double-breasted
brown suit.)*

RUFE
Milo Crawford.

OLIN
Milo.

MILO
Looky here, looky here. Ah caught this-here feller sneakin'
around outside the door!

L.D.
Let him go, Milo, this here is Lonnie Roy McNeil. He's a new
member.

MILO
A new member?

L.D.
Yes, damnit, a new member!

MILO
Well, gosh, ah didn't know.

RED
Well, you know now, you damned fool! So turn him loose!

MILO
(Releasing him.) Shucks ah'm plumb sorry, feller. Ah didn't
know.

LONNIE
That's okay.

COLONEL
What's goin' on?

L.D.
Nuthin', Colonel.

MILO
Shucks, Colonel, ah didn't know.

COLONEL
Who are you?

MILO
Milo Crawford, Colonel.

COLONEL
Ah thought you took your mama to Big Spring.

MILO
Couldn't get mah danged old pickup started.

OLIN
You try pumpin' her?

MILO
Yeah, but it didn't do no good. Ah jest don't seem to git no gas.

RUFE
Probable the fuel line.

MILO
Speck so.

OLIN
Or the carburetor . . .

L.D.
Well, anyway, since you're here now, go on over there and shake hands with Lonnie Roy McNeil.

MILO
(Shaking hands.) Pleased to meet you. How's come ah never seed you around affore? You new in town or somethin'?

LONNIE
No, sir. Ah live over to Silver City.

COLONEL
Silver City!

RUFE
(Covering up.) He's a helluva nice guy, Milo.

OLIN
He's old Grady McNeil's boy, Milo.

MILO
I see.

L.D.
Well, now that we all know each other, let's please, please, git on with the votin'.

MILO
What we votin' on?

L.D.
We're votin' on Lonnie Roy here.

COLONEL
Who?

RED
Lonnie Roy McNeil!!

COLONEL
Ah thought we already done that.

SKIP
We was, but Milo Crawford messed ever'thang up.

COLONEL
Milo Crawford? Ah thought he went over to Big Spring.

MILO
Ah couldn't get mah pickup started, Colonel.

COLONEL
You try pushin' her?

RUFE
Won't do no good to push her if she ain't gittin' any gas.

OLIN
Probable the carburetor.

MILO
Speck so.

RED
(Sarcastically) What happened to Mama, Milo? She gotta stay home all by herself tonight?

MILO
No. George and Jane Williams come by and give her a ride.

RED
Ooo-eee, ain't that nice!

SKIP
Let's git on with the votin'!

RUFE
Hell, yes. Let's git on with it.

L.D.
Okay, Okay. Lonnie Roy, would you please ... *(He indicates the door.)*

LONNIE
Shore thing. *(He goes out.)*

MILO
Where's he goin'?

L.D.
Outside.

MILO
Why?

L.D.
Rules.

MILO
Rules?

L.D., RED, OLIN, SKIP, AND RUFE
Rules!!!

MILO
I see.

L.D.
Okay. Ever'body wantin' Lonnie Roy McNeil for a new member, put up their hand. *(They all do except the* COLONEL.) What's wrong, Colonel, why ain't you votin'?

COLONEL
Votin'? What for?

L.D.
Go over and put up the Colonel's hand, will you, Red.

RED
Shore thing. *(He does.)*

COLONEL
What's goin' on? What's goin' on?

L.D.
Nuthin', Colonel. Red's jest helpin' you to vote, that's all.

COLONEL
Oh, well, thank you, Red. Damn nice of you.

RED
Mah pleasure, Colonel.

L.D.
Fine, fine. That's real official-like. Okay, Brother Knight Potts, you can bring in Lonnie Roy now.

OLIN
Okay. *(He opens the door.)* All right, Lonnie Roy, you-all can come in now. Lonnie Roy? Lonnie Roy? *(He steps outside.)* Well, what the hell!

L.D.
What's wrong?

OLIN
(Sticking his head back into the room.) He's gone.

(They all freeze in place as the lights fade to BLACKOUT.)

ACT II

The scene opens in the meeting room seconds later. The characters are found in positions held at the end of Act I. As the lights come up, they remain frozen for a moment before the dialogue begins.

L.D.
What the hell you mean, he's gone?

OLIN
He's gone, he ain't out here.

L.D.
Well, damnit, go look for him. See if Ramsey-Eyes saw where he went.

OLIN
Okay. *(He exits.)*

RED
Well, whattayou know about that.

L.D.
He'll be back, he didn't have no reason to run off or anythin'.

COLONEL
What's happened? What's goin' on?

SKIP
Lonnie Roy's gone, Colonel.

COLONEL
Gone? Gone where?

SKIP
We don't know, Colonel.

L.D.
He ain't gone, ah tell you.

RED
What kinda fellers you bringin' around here, Rufe? Runnin' away from an initiation.

RUFE
Well, hell, Red, ah don't know. He seemed like a nice-enough feller to me.

MILO
Ah didn't like the looks of him the first time ah laid eyes on him.

COLONEL
Shoot the son-of-a-bitch!

(There is a knock at the door.)

L.D.
Ah'll bet that's him now. You see, ah told you he never run off. Come in, Brother Elect Knight of the White Magnolia, *Lonnie Roy McNeil!*

(The door opens and RAMSEY-EYES *comes in.)*

RAMSEY-EYES
'Scuse me.

RED
What the hell you doin' up here!

RAMSEY-EYES
(Feisty) Mistah Olin Potts done told me to come up hyare and tell you iffen ah seed where Mistah Lonnie Roy McNeil went to!

L.D.
Well, did you?

RAMSEY-EYES
No, sah, but he never went out through de lobby 'cause ah been sittin' down dere by de door.

RUFE
Where's Olin now?

RAMSEY-EYES
He's gone over to see iffen Mistah Lonnie Roy McNeil went down and out de back way.

L.D.
Did the clerk see anythin'?

RAMSEY-EYES
No, sah, he didn't see nuthin' 'cause he's been asleep for 'most an hour. But not me, no, sah, ah been wide awake all evenin'.

COLONEL
Good man, Ramsey-Eyes.

RAMSEY-EYES
Ah been keepin' guard, Colonel Kinkaid, sah.

COLONEL
Damn good man.

RAMSEY-EYES
Thank you, sah.

COLONEL
Back on down to your post now, Ramsey-Eyes.

RAMSEY-EYES
Thank you, sah. Yes, sah. *(Exiting.)* Ah been wide awake all
evenin'.

RED
(Muttering) Stupid idiot wouldn't recognize Lonnie Roy if
he fell over him.

COLONEL
Faithful employee, that Ramsey-Eyes.

L.D.
Sure, Colonel, sure.

COLONEL
Ah would trust that man with anythin' ah owned. *(To* RUFE*)*
General Pershing once commanded Neegrow troops, betcha
didn't know that, did you?

RUFE
(Interested) No, Colonel, I didn't.

COLONEL
Montana territory, October 1895. Troop of the 10th Cavalry.
Neegrow troops. "Buffalo soldiers," the Injuns called 'em.

RUFE
Well, I'll be damned.

SKIP
Aw to hell with it, let's break open the booze.

RED
Gittin' a little shaky there, Skip?

SKIP
No, ah jest don't see any reason not to now.

RED
Whattayou think, L.D.?

L.D.
I don't know. It jest don't figger. You know that kid seemed interested, really interested.

RED
Yeah, well, seein' as how our hope for the future done vanished into thin air, let's drink to the one who got away. *(He takes one of the bottles out of the bag.)* Who's first?

*(*SKIP *reaches frantically for the bottle just as we hear a timid little knock at the door and* LONNIE ROY *sticks his head in the room.)*

LONNIE
Votin' all over with?

RED
Where the hell you been?

LONNIE
Ah hadda go pee.

SKIP
Jesus H. Christ on a crutch.

LONNIE
Well, ah hadda.

RED
Looks like we're gonna have an initiation after all, Skip.

SKIP
Aw, come on, Red, jest one shot, jest one.

RED
Sorry, Skip. Rules is rules.

LONNIE
Was ah voted in?

L.D.
You sure was, Lonnie Roy. Ever'body voted for you. Ain't that somethin'?

LONNIE
Well, ah am truly gratified.

L.D.
That jest shows you how much all the brothers think of you.

OLIN
(Entering.) Ah cain't find that stupid little son-of-a-bitch anywhere!

RUFE
He's here, Olin.

OLIN
Oh, yeah, well. Howdy there, Lonnie Roy.

LONNIE
Ah hadda go pee.

OLIN
Oh. Ah didn't think to look down the hall.

L.D.
Well, ever'thin' is all right now. Now we can have our initiation.

SKIP
It's about by-God time.

L.D.
(Who has been looking behind the podium.) Where's the book?

RED
What book?

L.D.
The initiation book. It ain't on the shelf behind the speaker's thing here.

RED
Well, don't look at me. I ain't got it.

L.D.
It's always been on this-here shelf, now it ain't. Now, who took it?

MILO
Ah ain't got it.

OLIN
Me neither.

L.D.
Skip?

SKIP
Are you kidding!

L.D.
Rufe?

RUFE
No, sir.

SKIP
What about the Colonel?

COLONEL
Who? What? What's goin' on?

L.D.
We're tryin' to find the initiation book, Colonel.

COLONEL
Well, go ahead and find it! Who the hell's stoppin' you?

L.D.
We was wonderin' if you had it, Colonel.

COLONEL
Had what?

RED
The goddamned initiation book!!!

COLONEL
Hell no, I ain't got no book!!

L.D.
(In a mild state of panic) Well—damn! How we gonna hold
a ceremony without a book?

SKIP
Let's jest make one up.

L.D.
What the hell you talkin' about?

SKIP
Make up our own ceremony. *(He stands in front of* LONNIE
ROY.*)* Hokus-pokus Maynard C. Stempco, get ready, get set,

Little Clete Spencer—zap! Lonnie Roy McNeil, you are now initiated. Let's have a drink.

MILO
That wouldn't be right. Lonnie Roy wouldn't be a proper member.

OLIN
No, sir, somethin' like that would be agin the rules.

SKIP
What rules?

RUFE
The rules of the order of the Knights of the White Magnolia, that's what rules.

SKIP
Well, hell, there ain't no Knights of the White Magnolia but us. So what difference does it make?

L.D.
It makes plenty of difference. That rule book was writ by Maynard C. Stempco himself, way back in 1902. It's got secret valuable writin's in it.

RUFE
Damn right.

L.D.
We gotta find that book.

RED
You sure it ain't back there on the shelf?

L.D.
It ain't here, I tell you. Only thing on this damned shelf is a box of dominoes.

RUFE
Maybe it's in the room some place.

(They all vaguely look around the room.)

L.D.
Well, look for it!

OLIN
Don't see it.

L.D.
Hell, it ain't in here either. Now hold on just a second, let's jest hold on and think a little bit. Now, who the hell was the last man we initiated?

OLIN
Milo Crawford.

L.D.
Milo, when was you initiated?

MILO
What year is this?

L.D.
It's still 1962.

SKIP
It's been that way ever since January, Milo.

MILO
In nineteen hundred and fifty-seven.

L.D.
You shore?

MILO
Yep, 'cause that's the year my mama had her nervous break-
down.

L.D.
Yeah, well, who did the book readin'?

MILO
You did.

L.D.
Oh yeah, ah spoze ah did.

RED
(Taunting) What'd you do with the book, L.D.?

COLONEL
What's goin' on?

SKIP
L.D. lost the initiation book, Colonel.

COLONEL
That was a damn-fool thing to do, L.D.

L.D.
Ah never lost nuthin'.

RUFE
Well, hell, L.D., you had it last.

LONNIE
Does this mean ah ain't gonna git initiated after all?

L.D.
Of course you're gonna git initiated. Soon as ah can think
where ah put that damn-fool book.

RED
Where'd you put it after you used it last?

L.D.
Ah thought ah put it on that shelf behind the speaker's outfit.

OLIN
Well, that jest messes up ever'thin'.

MILO
Shore does.

LONNIE
This mean ah ain't gonna git initiated after all?

SKIP
Hell, let's all have us a little drink, maybe it'll help us remember.

RED
Ah thought you drank to forgit.

SKIP
Forgit? Shore, ah drink to forgit, an' ah got plenty to forgit too. You know, the Colonel here ain't the only one that's seen fightin'. Ah seen it too, plenty of it.

RED
Shore you have.

SKIP
Ah have, ah tell you! Plenty of it! Over there in Ko-rea ah was in every combat sector there was.

RED
You never was in shit! That buddy of yours that married your sister told me you guys never got closer to any front lines than fifty miles.

SKIP
That ain't true.

L.D.
(Who has been deep in thought.) Wait a minute! Wait a minute. Ah remember now! Ah gave the book to the Colonel.

MILO
The Colonel?

L.D.
That's right, he asked me for it and ah gave it to him.

(They all turn and look at the COLONEL.*)*

COLONEL
(After a moment, very quietly) Ramsey-Eyes has it.

L.D.
What was that, Colonel?

COLONEL
(Louder) Ramsey-Eyes has it!

L.D.
What in the name of Christ is Ramsey-Eyes doin' with it?

COLONEL
He keeps it for me.

L.D.
Well, if that ain't the damnedest thing ah ever heard of in my life. You mean to tell me that you gave the Knights of the White Magnolia secret book to Ramsey-Eyes!

RED
Jeezus Christ!

COLONEL

No, ah didn't give it to him. Ah told you-all, ah jest let him keep it.

L.D.

What the hell for?

COLONEL

'Cause ah was afraid ah would lose it. Mah memory's been givin' me some troubles lately and ah didn't want to lose it.

L.D.

But why Ramsey-Eyes? Why not one of the brothers?

COLONEL

Because for one thing he is an old and faithful employee, and for another thing ah wouldn't trust any of you bumble-dicks with the rule book if it were writ on the side of an elephant!

RED

Well, ah'll be damned.

COLONEL

Probably.

L.D.

(Resigned) Olin, would you please go down to the lobby and ask Ramsey-Eyes for the book.

OLIN

Shore thing. *(He exits.)*

LONNIE

Does this mean ah'm gonna git initiated now?

L.D.

Yes, damnit, yes! Now sit down over there and shut up!

LONNIE
(Sitting.) Ah never done nuthin.

COLONEL
Bumble-dicks.

MILO
Gawlee, ah cain't git over it. Ramsey-Eyes, with the rule book.

RUFE
You reckin he read it?

RED
Hell, no!

SKIP
How you know?

RED
'Cause he's too damn dumb even to write his own name. Much less *read* anything.

RUFE
Well, at least we know where it is.

MILO
Yes, that's true. You know, even in the darkest moments you can always find a little good.

RUFE
(Impressed) By God, that's damn truthful, Milo.

MILO
Thank you.

RUFE
You orter write that one down some place and send it in to a magazine or somethin'.

MILO
Think so?

RUFE
Hell, yes. Whattayou think, Red?

RED
Who gives a damn!

SKIP
Why don't you write it on the shithouse wall over to Red's place?

L.D.
Shut up, Skip.

COLONEL
"Shut up, Kinkaid," that's what old Black Jack said when we was out there in Mexico. Hot as hell one day there in the officers' mess. Wind blowin' the tent sides back and forth. Flap, flap, flap . . .

OLIN
(Entering.) Well, here it is. He had it in an old seegar box in a closet.

L.D.
(Taking the book.) That's the damnedest thing ah ever heard in my life.

RED
Crazy old fool.

L.D.
Okay, boys, let's git at it. *(Walks to the podium and opens the book.)* Okay. Now, Red, you come up here and stand by me. Now, Milo, you stand by the station of the moon. Olin, you stand by the station of the sun, and, Rufe, you stand by the

station of the west wind. Let's see now, what part can we give
the Colonel?

COLONEL
Don't want no part. Ah don't feel good. Ah got me a head-
ache.

OLIN
You want ah should go down and git you an aspirin, Colonel?

COLONEL
Don't want no part.

RED
Forgit him. Let's git on with it.

COLONEL
Ah was havin' me a cup of coffee with the Major when old
Black Jack come in. Well, sir, as luck would have it, he come
in jest as I was sayin' to the Major, "Ah don't think we're ever
gonna catch that fat little greaser if we stay out here in this
damn Meheeko for five hundred years . . ." and the General
he says to me he says . . . *(Voice trails off.)*

L.D.
Lonnie Roy, you stand in front of Red and me.

LONNIE
Yes, sir.

L.D.
Okay, Skip. You hand out the written parts.

SKIP
Right.

LONNIE
(To RED*)* Boy, this is excitin', ain't it?

RED
(Muttering) If you like hunred-year-old snatch, it's a gas.

(L.D. *takes some cards out of the book and hands them to*
SKIP. SKIP *walks around handing out the written roles
while* L.D. *takes the initiation hats out of the trunk. The
hats are fez-type with ribbons on the back and emblems
on the front. A half moon, a sunburst, a cloud with
streamers for the west wind, a lamp for wisdom, a series
of fountain-type lines for the truth, and a bolt of light-
ning for the wizard.)*

L.D.
Now, Brothers, here are the *Chapeaux de rituale*. Milo, you
are the moon. Olin, you are the sun. Rufe, you are the west
wind. Skip, you are Wisdom the Guide to the Mystic Mountain.

SKIP
Hot damn.

L.D.
Red, you are the Golden Fountain of Truth and ah am the
Imperial Wizard.

*(The knights put on their hats and move back to their sta-
tions looking over their roles. As they are doing this, the*
COLONEL *says his lines.)*

COLONEL
Flap, flap, flap. Horses standin' round hip-shot, slappin' at
flies with their tails, lots of flies buzzin' around.

OLIN
Hey, L.D., somethin's wrong with my hat.

L.D.
Spin it around, Olin, you got it on backward.

RUFE
Hey, look at old Milo Crawford there.

(MILO*'s hat is much too big and is almost down over his ears.*)

L.D.
Milo, put that thing on the back of your head, you look like hell.

SKIP
Hey, Red, that thing you got on your head look a whole lot like somethin' ah got growin' on my butt.

RED
Go to hell!

L.D.
Shut up, Skip!

RUFE
Ah cain't read my part.

L.D.
Why the hell not?

RUFE
It's got a big splotch or somethin' right in the middle of it.

L.D.
Well, read around the goddamn splotch!

RUFE
(Dubiously) Okay.

L.D.
Okay now, here we go. *(He starts to read.)* "You are now on

a journey, initiate Lonnie Roy McNeil. A journey to seek the Golden Fountain of Truth that flows deep in the darkness of the Mystic Mountain."

LONNIE
Gawlee.

L.D.
During your journey, initiate Lonnie Roy McNeil, you will converse with the great heavenly sages, and as you heed their advice, your reply will be "Stempco, Stempco, Stempco." Do you understand?

LONNIE
Stempco, Stempco, Stempco. Yes, sir.

L.D.
But you are not alone, initiate Lonnie Roy McNeil. By your decision to become a Knight of the White Magnolia you have wisdom by your side to guide you toward truth.

SKIP
(Reading) "Ah am wisdom. Ah am with you always as your friend and companion. Fear not as we begin our journey, for ah am here with you to place your footsteps on the right path toward truth."

LONNIE
Stempco, Stempco, Stempco.

L.D.
Your first journey, initiate *Lonnie Roy McNeil,* is to the pale-blue grotto of the moon.

(SKIP *leads* LONNIE ROY *over to* MILO.)

MILO
(Reading) "Ah am the moon. By night ah cast beams down

upon you, lightin' the way along your journey toward the truth."

LONNIE
Stempco, Stempco, Stempco.

L.D.
You now travel, initiate Lonnie Roy McNeil, to the blazin' realm of the sun.

*(*SKIP *leads* LONNIE ROY *to* OLIN.*)*

OLIN
"Ah am the sun. Ah bring my warmin' rays and glorious beams to warm and comfort you durin' the day as you journey toward the truth."

LONNIE
Stempco, Stempco, Stempco.

L.D.
You now travel, initiate Lonnie Roy McNeil, to the long low plains of the west wind.

*(*SKIP *leads him to* RUFE.*)*

COLONEL
Flap, flap, flap . . .

RUFE
(Reading with great difficulty.) "Ah am the west w_____. Ah blow my balmy bree_____ er _____ the _____ren desert an_____ the sails of your craf_____ cross the sea of ignor_____ on your journey toward the truth. Hell, L.D., it don't make no sense readin' around this-here splotch.

L.D.
It sounded jest fine, Rufe. Anyway, we got the idea.

COLONEL
Flap, flap, flap . . .

L.D.
You now arrive, initiate Lonnie Roy McNeil, at the Mystic Mountain, wherein lies the Golden Fountain of Truth and the great white marble temple of the Imperial Wizard.

(SKIP brings LONNIE ROY to the podium and has him kneel down.)

RED
(Starting to read) "Ah am the Golden . . ." *(Just as he reads the COLONEL says the role from memory.)*

COLONEL
"Ah am the Golden Fountain of Truth. I welcome travelers to my magic waters. Your journey has been long and hard, but rejoice now, pilgrim, your reward is at hand."

LONNIE
Stempco, Stempco, Stempco.

L.D.
By God, Colonel, that was real fine. How was it, Red?

RED
(Grinning.) Letter-perfect.

L.D.
Jesus, Colonel. You think you can remember the part of the Imperial Wizard too?

COLONEL
Shut your mouth, Lieutenant Kinkaid. You keep talkin' a lot of bull and I'll have you on the horseshit detail for the rest of the campaign.

RED
Offhand, L.D., ah'd say that wasn't it.

L.D.
Yes, well, maybe ah'd better read it. "Ah am the Imperial Wizard. You have been guided by wisdom and aided by the sun, the moon, and the west wind to taste now the living waters of the Golden Fountain of Truth." Oh hell!

RED
What's wrong?

L.D.
It says here that ah am now to give the initiate a drink of clear water from a silver cup. Ah forgot all about that.

OLIN
Ah could go down to the lobby for a Coke.

RED
How about a shot of booze?

MILO
That's what you gave me when ah was initiated.

RED
Did you take it?

MILO
Of course ah took it.

RED
Does your mama know about this?

MILO
Ah do lots of things my mama don't know about.

RED
Shore you do.

L.D.
Okay, okay, let's do this right now. Give Lonnie Roy the bottle, Red.

RED
Okay. *(Opens the bottle, hands it to* LONNIE ROY.*)*

L.D.
Let's see. Uh . . . Living waters of the Golden Fountain of Truth. Drink deeply, knight initiate Lonnie Roy McNeil, your quest has been rewarded.

*(*LONNIE ROY *takes a long pull.)*

RED
(Grabbing the bottle.) Not too damn deeply.

SKIP
How about a shot for his faithful companion?

L.D.
Shut up, Skip. Now that you have known wisdom and tasted truth, knight initiate Lonnie Roy McNeil, you are ready to receive the final rites of membership. Light up the cross, Olin.

OLIN
Okay. *(He flips on the switch by the door. The cross comes on but the bulbs are so covered with dust, dirt, and fly specks that they are barely visible.)*

L.D.
What's wrong with that damn thing?

OLIN
Sure seems dim-like.

RUFE

I'll jiggle it a little bit and maybe it'll come on better. *(He walks over to the cross and looks at it.)* Well, no damn wonder!

L.D.

What's wrong?

RUFE

Well, it's all covered with dust and stuff.

L.D.

Well, git somethin' and clean it off.

RUFE

Turn off the light, Olin. *(He pulls a chair over and stands on it to clean the bulbs with his handkerchief.* MILO, RED, *and* OLIN *gather around to help him.)*

COLONEL

When General Pershing was a lieutenant, he was instructin' all them smarty-assed Kay-dets there at the West Point and they didn't like him. No, sir, they did not like him one little bit. So when they found out that he commanded them Nee-grow troops, they started callin' him Black Jack.

MILO

. . . Spit on the base affore you screw it back in.

RED

Somebody orter spit on your base.

COLONEL

But he fixed 'em. He jest held on to the name, you see. Made it famous, by God. Yes, sir, you can have your goddamn Ike's and Doug's, give me old Black Jack Pershing anytime. Yes, sir!

OLIN

Don't touch them wires there . . . they'll shock the hell outta
you.

RUFE

How can they shock me? You got the switch turned off, ain't
you?

OLIN

Shore I got it off, but don't you know electricity lingers.

RUFE

Electricity lingers . . . that's the dumbest thing I ever heard
in mah life.

L.D.

For Christ's sake, ain't you all finished yet?

RUFE

All done, L.D. Okay, Olin, you can fire it up again.

(OLIN *does—the cross gleams more or less like new.*)

L.D.

That's a lot better. Okay, Olin, you can turn off the room
lights now.

(OLIN *does. They all stand in the dim glow of the cross.*)

LONNIE

Gee, that's pretty.

OLIN

Ain't that somethin'!

MILO

It looks like church or somethin'. You know?

COLONEL
What's that glow up there? What is it?

L.D.
We got the cross on, Colonel.

COLONEL
Used to fire them lights up in the sky over the trenches. Light
things up real bright like, then commence to shootin'. Hated
them damn lights.

RED
You and General Pershing right, Colonel?

COLONEL
General Pershing? He told me to shut up one time. You
know, he never said anythin' to me again, not one word, 'cept
maybe to give an order or two. Ah don't think he liked me.

L.D.
Shore, Colonel, shore. Now, Brother Knights, we come to the
most important part of our initiation. This-here part ah'm
about to read to you, Lonnie Roy McNeil, is the real meanin'
of White Magnoliaism . . . *(The cross makes a few sputtering
noises and goes out, plunging the room into darkness.)* What
the hell? Turn on the lights, Olin.

OLIN
Ah'm gittin' there.

(The lights go on.)

L.D.
Rufe, see if you can fix that damn thing.

RUFE
Hell, ah don't know what's wrong with it, L.D. It must have
a short in it or somethin'.

L.D.
Well, quit foolin' with it. We'll go on without it.

COLONEL
Don't like the goddamn dark!

RED
Git on with it, L.D. Ah'm gittin' tired of standin' here.

SKIP
Me too. Can't we git Lonnie Roy sworn in sittin' down? *(He sits down.)*

L.D.
Hell no, Skip!

MILO
Confound it, Skip, you're gonna ruin the whole darn thing.

SKIP
Hell with it. Ah done my part. Guided old Lonnie Roy here plumb to the Mystic Mountain an' ah'm bushed. Besides that, my piles itch. *(He squirms around in the chair.)*

L.D.
Goddamnit, Skip, stand up!

COLONEL
Gits goddamn dark in the trenches, ah can tell you. The rats come out in the dark and eat up ever'thin' they can git their teeth into.

RUFE
(Sits down.) Aw, the hell with it!

MILO
Now, come on, fellers, it won't hurt you none to stand up a little while longer so's we can git Lonnie Roy sworn in proper.

COLONEL

Them rats was fat too. Big and fat, that's 'cause there was so many bodies to eat on, you see, and the fellers used to say that if one of them rats breathed on you that you would die! That's right, they would come up at night and breathe on you, then they would commence eatin' on your body. That's right. That's right!

OLIN

Hey, Colonel, take it easy. Boy, ah don't know, L.D., he's really got snakes in his boots tonight.

L.D.

He'll be okay, jest leave him alone, Olin.

LONNIE

What's wrong with him? He crazy or somethin'?

L.D.

No, no, of course not, he jest has these spells. Now, please, will ever'body sit down.

OLIN

Me too?

L.D.

You too.

OLIN

About by-God time.

RED

(Moving off platform.) Ah wish to hell you'd make up your damn mind.

L.D.

Well, it is made up. Ah want ever'body sittin'.

(LONNIE ROY makes a move for the chair.)

Damnit, Lonnie Roy, not you!

LONNIE
Mah knees hurt.

L.D.
Well, that's too bad. *You* gotta kneel down there.

LONNIE
Yes, sir.

SKIP
For Christ's sake, let's git this damn thing over with and have a drink!

RED
Why the hell don't you shut up, you goddamn little lush. You'll get a drink when ever'body else does and not until then!

SKIP
Ah'm not a lush, damn you, ah'm not! Who the hell do you think you're talkin' to anyway?

RED
Oh sure, ah plumb forgot. You're a hero, ain't you? A Korean war hero.

SKIP
Ah seen plenty of stuff over there, lot more than the Colonel ever seen; ah been in battles, big battles.

RED
Shore, shore. The battle of the Tattoo Parlor and the Beer Hall. Face it, Skip, you're nuthin' but a phony, a boozer and a phony.

SKIP
Ah'm not, damn you! Ah'm not!

L.D.
All right now, all right, that's jest a goddamn nuff! This part
I'm about to read is real important and ah want it quiet in
here!

*(The cross light comes on again, this time very bright and
vivid, then it goes off.)*

RUFE
Mah Gawd, did you see that!

COLONEL
What was that? What was that flash?

L.D.
Nuthin', Colonel, just that damn-fool cross actin' up again.

(Cross sputters on and off.)

COLONEL
A creepin' barrage. *Five-nines* and *seventy-sevens,* blowin'
up all around us! Throwin' up bodies of Frenchmen that was
killed over a year before. Old bodies and new bodies jumbled
together in the air.

SKIP
(Getting up and moving away.) Mah God, listen to that! For
Christ's sake, somebody shut him up!

(Cross sputters on and off.)

COLONEL
(His voice rising to a high whine) Hangin' on the old bob
wire like pieces of pork. Fellers out there with half their guts
shot away, sharin' a shell hole with a year-old corpse, out
there all night screamin' and cryin' on the old bob wire.

RUFE
(In a hushed voice) Mah God, ah ain't never heard him talk this crazy-like affore.

(The cross light flares on and off again.)

COLONEL
Stop that, stop doin' that! Cain't you see ah'm old now? Ah'm old, ah'm an old man! Ah'm not like ah was. Ah was young then. Ah was young when ah was in France. Ah could be with wimmen. Walkin' down them streets of Bar-le-Duc like some kind of young god, American Doughboy, six foot tall. Oh, God. Oh, mah God. What's wrong with me?

SKIP
(Going to him.) Colonel Kinkaid? Colonel Kinkaid, for God's sake, stop it! Snap out of it!

COLONEL
Who is that? Who's got hold of me? Is that you, George?

SKIP
No, Colonel, it's . . .

COLONEL
Is that you, George Plummer? Remember when we was at the Argonne. Them dirty bastards killed you there, didn't they, George Plummer? You was afraid and that goddamned whiz-bang hit and tore off your head, and your body jumped up and run off like it was still alive, flappin' its arms and runnin' and the boys next to me shootin' at it, shootin' at it, shootin' at it for the hell of it, shootin' and laughin' and your head rollin' around on the duckboards at the bottom of the trench like some kind of ball.

SKIP
He's gone crazy, it's like he was still over there. Still fightin' that old war.

RED

Doesn't sound too heroic when it's the real thing, does it, hot shot!

(Cross sputters on and off.)

RUFE

Maybe we better git him outta here.

L.D.

Olin, you better go on down to the lobby and git Ramsey-Eyes to phone over to the Colonel's house and tell Floyd to come on over here and pick up his daddy.

OLIN

Shore thing. *(He exits.)*

(Cross sputters on and off.)

COLONEL

Killin' people all around me! Throwin' the bodies up in the air! Up in the air.

L.D.

Shore, Colonel, shore.

LONNIE

We gonna have the rest of the readin' soon?

L.D.

The what? Oh, shore, shore, Lonnie Roy, of course we are.

LONNIE

Shore seems like a long time.

COLONEL

The padre come along and put that head in a sack. It musta

been a flour sack or somethin', 'cause when he walked, it let out little puffs of smoke and the blood run out over his shoes and over his . . . over his puttees. One of the boys yelled out, "Hey, Padre, you're gettin' maggots in the gravy." Hey, Padre, you're gettin' mag . . . mag . . . oh, mah God!

SKIP

Jesus Christ, now that's enough. *(Backing away.)* That's enough!

RED

Maybe a shot of whiskey would help him.

L.D.

Damn good idea, Red. Bring that bottle over here.

RUFE

Why don't you jest leave him be?

L.D.

Ah'll hold his head back and you give him a drink.

RED.

Okay. *(L.D. holds the* COLONEL*'s head back and* RED *puts the bottle to the* COLONEL*'s lips. The* COLONEL *thrashes about violently and spits the fluid out all over* RED*'s shirt.)* Look here what he done to my shirt.

COLONEL

Let me go, let me go. Ah ain't crazy, damn you! It's jest them shells. Oh, Jesus, they're comin', the Germans. Oh, Jesus God, ah can see their shadows up agin the wire.

RED

Goddamn crazy old fool, look what he done to my shirt!

OLIN
(Entering.) Ramsey-Eyes is phonin' over to Floyd's now.

RED
Damnit to hell, this is a bran'-new shirt.

RUFE
Serves you right. Ah told you to leave him alone.

RED
Keep your damn trap shut, Rufe. Who the hell asked you anythin'.

OLIN
Now hold on here. There ain't no call for you to go yellin' at Rufe.

RED
Ah'll yell at anybody ah damn well want to!

SKIP
To hell with this, ah need a drink! *(He grabs bottle.)*

RED
Put down that bottle, Skip.

SKIP
Go to hell, ah need this!

RED
Gimme that bottle or ah'll break your goddamn neck!

SKIP
(Pulling an object from his pocket and concealing it with his hand.) If you think you can git by this-here knife, you jest come on ahead!

LONNIE
(Jumping away.) Jesus God, he's got him a knife!

L.D.
Don't be a damn fool, Skip. Come on and give us the knife, then you can have all you want to drink.

SKIP
Ah got all ah want right now. *(He takes a long drink.)*

RED
You rotten little bastard! You stinkin' two-bit lush!

SKIP
Stay where you are, Red, or ah'll cut you! Ah ain't kiddin' now.

RUFE
(Backing away.) Watch him, Red, watch him.

MILO
Maybe we'd better adjourn this-here meetin' and finish off the initiation next time.

COLONEL
(Grabbing hold of LONNIE ROY, *who has backed into his wheelchair.)* Help me, help me. God in heaven, help me.

LONNIE
(Screams and struggles to get loose.) He's got me! He's got me! Old crazy man's got me! Old crazy man's got me, help, help. *(He tears loose from the* COLONEL *and bolts out the door. The* COLONEL *slumps over in his chair.)*

L.D.
Stop him, Olin, don't let him get away!

OLIN
Come on, Rufe.

(They dash out the door after LONNIE ROY.*)*

RED
To hell with him. Help me git the knife away from Skip.

L.D.
Come on now, Skip. Give me that knife.

SKIP
(Hands L.D. *a small tire gauge and grins.)* What knife?

L.D.
Damn tire gauge!

RED
(Advances on SKIP *swiftly.)* You son-of-a-bitch! *(He grabs the bottle from* SKIP *and smashes him viciously in the stomach.* SKIP *doubles up and falls to the floor.)*

SKIP
Oh, my gut. Damn you, Red, ah think ah'm gonna puke.

RED
(Pulling him up.) Not in here you ain't. *(He opens the door and pushes* SKIP *out.)* Git your ass on down the hall. *(*RED *comes back in and closes the door.)* Half a bottle. That damn little sot drank half a bottle.

MILO
Well, ah think it's time for me to be gittin' on home now.

L.D.
No! By God, you stay right where you are, Milo.

MILO
Gee, L.D., it's gittin' late and you know my mother waits up for me on meetin' nights.

L.D.
Screw your mother! You're stayin' right here till Olin and Rufe git back with Lonnie Roy.

MILO
(Shocked) What did you say about my mother?

L.D.
Nuthin', Milo. Ah mean, ah didn't mean to say it.

MILO
You had no call to say somethin' like that. No call at all, now, by gollies, you apologize, L.D. You jest apologize for sayin' that!

RED
Go to hell! L.D. here ain't apologizin' for nuthin'.

L.D.
Now wait a minute, Red . . .

MILO
Well, he better! He jest better or ah'm walkin' out that-there door an' never comin' back!

RED
Well, go ahead and walk damnit. Who the hell needs you. Stinkin' little mama's boy!

L.D.
Now hold on a minute, Red. Wait, Milo, don't go.

MILO
Well, ah'm goin'. Ah'm goin' right now!

RED
You bet your ass you are. Git!!!

(MILO exits, then returns suddenly.)

MILO
Ah never did like you, Red Grover, never! You're nuthin' but a lard-butted booze drinker. *(He exits.)*

RED
(Laughing) "Lard-butted booze drinker." By God, ah've been called worse.

L.D.
You had no call to do that.

RED
Do what?

L.D.
Treat Milo thataway.

RED
Well, hell, L.D., you're the one that told him to go hump his own mother.

L.D.
Ah didn't mean that, but you did. You meant to run him off.

RED
So damn what. Ah never liked the gutless little s.o.b. anyway.

L.D.
But we need him. We need ever'body, don't you see? Jesus, we're breakin' up. Jest when things are startin' to look good, we start breakin' up.

(RUFE and OLIN enter.)

RUFE
Well, he's gone.

L.D.
You couldn't catch him, huh?

OLIN
The way that boy was runnin', he's probable back in Silver City by now.

RUFE
(Sitting down.) Olin and me is gittin' too old to run all over Bradleyville after half-initiated kids.

OLIN
(Seeing COLONEL.*)* What's wrong with the Colonel?

L.D.
(Rushing to COLONEL.*)* Oh, mah God! Colonel Kinkaid, are you okay? Colonel Kinkaid?

*(*OLIN *and* RUFE *gather around.)*

OLIN
Is he dead?

L.D.
(Feeling COLONEL*'s pulse.)* No, his heart's still beatin', but, mah God, he looks terrible. Olin, you and Rufe better git him on down to the lobby and wait with him till Floyd gits here.

RUFE
Okay, L.D. Come on, Olin. We'll wheel him to the stairs and carry him on down from there. *(He wheels the* COLONEL *out the door.* L.D. *watches them for a moment and then closes the door.)*

RED
Well, sir, that about does it.

L.D.
Yeah, ah guess the meetin's over all right. *(Starting to collect hats.)* Now, look here, that damn-fool Milo Crawford ran outta here with his moon hat on.

RED
No, ah don't mean the meetin'. Ah mean the whole shootin' match. There ain't gonna be any more meetin's.

L.D.
You're crazy!

RED
Ah am, huh?

L.D.
Yes. We ain't through by a long shot.

RED
Sure we are, L.D. That old man down there's gonna die. Ah can tell by lookin' at him, and with him dead there goes the old meetin' room. Like ah told you before, Floyd ain't gonna give nuthin' free to nobody.

L.D.
So what? That don't mean nuthin'. We can meet somewheres else. Hell's fire, the brotherhood means more than jest a beat-up old room in a flea-bag hotel.

RED
The *brotherhood?* Oh, mah God! The *"brotherhood!"* Jesus Christ, L.D., wake up. Git back on the goddamn planet. The *brotherhood* ain't any more. The *brotherhood* ran outta here with Lonnie Roy and Milo. The *brotherhood* fell on its ass

with Skip over there. The *brotherhood* got carried outta here with a dyin' old man. There ain't gonna be no stinkin' Knights of the White Magnolia cause the Knights of the White Magnolia idea is gone, finished, all washed up. Did you really listen to that crap we were readin' tonight? The Gospel according to Maynard C. Stempco. The sun, the moon, and the west wind? Well, L.D., old pal, lemme tell you as far as this-here lodge is concerned, the sun's done set, the moon's gone down, and the west wind's got a big splotch on it.

L.D.
That ain't true! The ideas that this-here lodge was founded on have a hell of a lot of meanin'.

RED
Meanin'? Meanin' to who? For God's sake, take a look around you, L.D., whatta ya see? Domino players, stumble bums, mama's boys, pimple-faced kids, and crazy old men.

L.D.
And you? Just where the hell do you fit in?

RED
Me? Ah don't fit in nowhere. Ah'm just a lard-butted booze drinker. Remember? *(He picks up the sack of whiskey.)* So I guess that jest leaves you, L.D. The only true believer, L. D. Alexander, supermarket manager and keeper of the White Magnolias. Let me tell you somethin', Brother White Knight, Imperial Wizard, you don't put down the sons-of-bitchin' freedom riders and minority bastards with all this crap any more. You got to look for the loopholes, pal. Let 'em all squawk about lunchrooms and schools all they want. In mah place ah simply reserve the right to refuse service to anybody. You look for the loopholes, pal. Well, so long, L.D. If ah don't see you down to the bar, ah'll save a seat for you on the back of the bus. *(He pitches the half-empty pint to him and exits, leaving the door open.)*

(L.D. watches him off and glances dejectedly around. Crosses to the door and closes it, then to the Stempco portrait and contemplates a moment, then he crosses to the truth banner, and after a moment rips it down and tosses it into the trunk. He takes off his hat and throws it into the trunk as well. The sound of a train passing through town makes him pause. The door opens and SKIP *comes in.)*

SKIP

Jesus, ah think he busted mah gut. Ah been pukin' up Dixie Dinette chiliburgers by the goddamn bucketful.

L.D.

(Giving SKIP *the bottle.)* Here, maybe this will help.

SKIP

Oh, God, thanks. *(He drinks.)* Where the hell is ever'body?

L.D.

Gone.

SKIP

Gone? Gone where?

L.D.

Quit. Walked out.

SKIP

Quit? Who quit?

L.D.

Lonnie Roy, Milo, and Red.

SKIP

What about the rest of the guys?

L.D.

Finished. It's all finished.

SKIP
(Getting up.) You mean Colonel Kinkaid quit too?

L.D.
You might say so, yes.

SKIP
Well, ah'll be damned.

(OLIN and RUFE re-enter.)

RUFE
Well, Floyd finally got here.

OLIN
He said he was gonna take his daddy straight over to Doc
Crowley's. He was mad as hell at us for lettin' the Colonel get
into that shape.

RUFE
That's right. He says he's gonna shut down the meetin' room.

L.D.
Let him go ahead. It don't matter no more anyway.

OLIN
Well, hell, L.D., if we cain't come up here no more, where
we gonna hold our meetin's?

L.D.
Whattayou care? What the hell do you come to the meetin's
for anyway?

OLIN
Well, hell, L.D., me and Rufe like to play the domino games
and Skip there, he, well, uh . . .

L.D.
Shore, shore, we all know why Skip comes up here.

SKIP

Now wait a minute. Ah never done nuthin'.

RUFE

Well, hell, L.D., we cain't jest quit.

L.D.

Who says we cain't? Ah'm tired of tryin' to keep ever'thin'
goin' any more. Watchin' things bust apart. Things ain't the
same no more. Damn, damn, things is changin'. Damn. Oh,
to hell with it. *(He walks to the podium and picks up the
initiation book.)* This-here lodge, this-here society, this-here
brotherhood, this-here ever'thin' is now adjourned! *(He takes
the book and slowly walks out.)*

OLIN

Well, what the hell do you think about that?

RUFE

What did he mean, "This-here brotherhood is now adjourned"?

SKIP

Ah think we jest knighted our last Magnolia, boys. All the rest
of the brothers done flew the coop.

RUFE

You mean that we're all the members there is?

SKIP

That's right. Who would have thought that one day old Olin
Potts there would be the Grand Imperial Wizard of the
White Magnolia? Stempco! Stempco! Stempco!

RUFE

Doggone it, ah'm sure gonna miss our old meetin' nights.

SKIP

Oh hell, yes, me too. Especially this last one. *(He rubs his stomach.)*

RUFE

Now there won't be nuthin' to do.

OLIN

Aw hell, Rufe, there's always somethin' to do. We could go over there to the new bowlin' alley and give that a try.

RUFE

Yeah, I spoze we could. Well, ah gotta be gittin' on back home now or Sara Beth will be mad as hell.

OLIN

Not half as mad as old Mabel's gonna be at me.

RUFE

What the hell you talkin' about, Olin? You know damn well Sara Beth can git a hunred times madder than Mabel ever could.

OLIN

Now listen here, Rufe Phelps, that ain't true.

RUFE

The hell it ain't. Old Sara Beth gits up in the morning mad at the rooster an' goes to bed at night cussin' the owl.

(They exit arguing. SKIP *watches the exit and finishes the rest of the bottle. He flips the bottle cap.* RAMSEY-EYES *enters.)*

RAMSEY-EYES

Meetin' all over with, Mistah Skip?

SKIP

Yes, Ramsey-Eyes, the meetin' is all over.

RAMSEY-EYES
Ah'll jest straighten thangs up and lock de door.

SKIP
You jest do that little old thing, Ramsey-Eyes. *(He looks at the empty bottle.)* Christ, ah wish ah had another drink.

RAMSEY-EYES
Mistah Red Grover is over to his saloon. Ah seed him go over dere when he left the hotel here.

SKIP
Hot damn! Ah'll bet he'll give me a drink, sure enough, ah jest bet he will. Thanks, Ramsey-Eyes. Good night. *(He exits.)*

RAMSEY-EYES
Good night, Mistah Skip. *(He closes the door and snaps the cross light switch a couple of times. When it doesn't work, he moves to the cross and raps the wall next to it with the broom handle. The cross lights up. He chuckles and moves back to the door, turning off the overhead lights. A piece of paper catches his eye. He picks it up and moves to the light of the cross to read.)* "Ah am de moon. By night ah cast beams down upon you, lightin' your way along your journey toward de truth." *(He chuckles.)* "Ah am de moon." Oh, Lawdy. "Ah am de moon." *(He chuckles again.)*

(The cross lights fade to BLACKOUT.*)*

Lu Ann Hampton Laverty Oberlander

Characters

LU ANN HAMPTON

SKIP HAMPTON

CLAUDINE HAMPTON

BILLY BOB WORTMAN

DALE LAVERTY

RED GROVER

RUFE PHELPS

OLIN POTTS

CORKY OBERLANDER

MILO CRAWFORD

CHARMAINE

ACT I

The time is 1953. The act is set in the living room of CLAUDINE *and* LU ANN HAMPTON*'s home in Bradleyville. A small frame house in a small frame town. The room is modestly furnished in Sears-catalogue-type furniture—sofa, table, chairs, radio, etc. A door upstage left leads to the kitchen. Upstage center door leads to bedrooms. Stage right is a small front porch section with a functional screen door.*

As the scene opens, CLAUDINE *slams through the kitchen door with bowl of tangerines, sets it on end table. She is a heavy-set woman in her early forties, her hair is grayish blond. She is dressed in house dress and apron—takes apron off and puts it on sofa back. Notes time and looks out porch door, then goes upstairs, picking up sneakers from landing.* LU ANN *runs on and into living room. She is dressed in the blue-and-gold uniform of a Bradleyville cheerleader. She is well built and very blond. She is also very pretty. Small-town pretty, healthy pretty, clean pretty, Pepsodent and Ivory Soap pretty.*

BILLY BOB
(Offstage) Lu Ann! Lu Ann! Wait up, will ya! *(Following* LU ANN *on.* BILLY BOB WORTMAN *is tall and lanky. He wears a white shirt, Levi's, boots, and a letter sweater. His crew-cut hair has been dyed green.)*

LU ANN
Ma! I'm home!

CLAUDINE
(Offstage) About time!

LU ANN
Well, ah thought ah would die! Ah jest thought ah would curl
up and die right there on the gym floor. When the coach
introduced the basketball team and you-all come out there
with your hair all dyed green. Well, sir, mah eyes liked to
jumped plumb outta mah head! Why, Mary Beth Johnson jest
hollered. That's right, jest hollered right out loud.

BILLY BOB
It was Pete Honeycutt's idea.

LU ANN
Why, ever'one jest laughed and shouted and carried on so.
Eveline Blair came runnin' over to me shoutin', "Look at the
basketball boys, look at the basketball boys!"

BILLY BOB
It was Pete Honeycutt's idea.

LU ANN
(Gestures to porch—they go out.) After the assembly we
cheerleaders all got together and decided we'd do somethin'
funny too.

BILLY BOB
Aw, like what?

LU ANN
Now wouldn't you like to know? Mr. Green-headed Billy Bob
Wortman.

BILLY BOB
Aw, come on, Lu Ann, what are you-all fixin' to do?

LU ANN
Oh, ah don't know, somethin', somethin' real neat.

BILLY BOB
You cain't dye you-all's hair. Pete Honeycutt already thought that one up.

LU ANN
Eveline Blair thought up different shoes.

BILLY BOB
Different shoes?

LU ANN
You know, come to school wearin' one high-heel shoe and one saddle shoe. Somethin' *neato* like that.

BILLY BOB
Yeah.

LU ANN
Ah don't know, though, it might be kinda tricky doin' the Locomotive in a high-heel shoe.

BILLY BOB
Might be at that.

LU ANN
But it might be fun.

BILLY BOB
Shore.

LU ANN
(Sitting on swing.) Maybe we can wear them out to the senior picnic.

BILLY BOB
(Joins her.) Shore!

LU ANN
We're still goin' in your daddy's Hudson, ain't we?

BILLY BOB
Well, uh, naw, we gotta use the pickup.

LU ANN
The pickup!

BILLY BOB
Yeah, my dad wants the car to go over to Big Spring.

LU ANN
But it's the senior picnic! Mah God, ah don't want to go to mah one and only senior picnic in a danged-old pickup.

BILLY BOB
Well, goshalmighty, Lu Ann, ah cain't help it.

LU ANN
What the heck good is it for your dad to have a bran'-new, step-down Hudson Hornet if *we* never get to use the danged old thing.

BILLY BOB
Seems like ever'thin' ah do is wrong.

LU ANN
Boy, that's the truth.

BILLY BOB
Gawlee, Ruthie Lee Lawell and Pete Honeycutt are goin' in his pickup.

LU ANN
So what.

BILLY BOB

Well, nuthin', ah jest mean that it don't seem to bother Ruthie Lee none.

LU ANN

Heck no, it don't bother Ruthie Lee none. Mah Gawd, she almost lives in Pete Honeycutt's pickup seat. I'll bet her bra spends more time on the danged gear shift than it spends on her.

BILLY BOB

(Shocked) Lu Ann Hampton! You know that ain't true.

LU ANN

It is so, too. I seen 'em when they was parked out to the drive-in and she was danged near naked.

BILLY BOB

I never saw nuthin'.

LU ANN

'Course you never saw nuthin'. You was too busy watchin' the movie. Mah Gawd, you was more worried about old Gary Cooper than Grace Kelly was.

BILLY BOB

Ah liked that movie.

LU ANN

Boy, you shore did.

BILLY BOB

Well, ah did.

LU ANN

No wonder Ruthie Lee has so many chest colds in the wintertime.

BILLY BOB
If Pete and Ruthie Lee was actin' like the way you said, that jest means they don't have any respect for each other.

LU ANN
Or for Gary Cooper.

BILLY BOB
Reverend Stone says that goin' on like that is a sinful sign of no respect.

LU ANN
Oh, brother.

BILLY BOB
People that behave thataway out to drive-ins and such-like is behavin' plumb un-Christian.

LU ANN
Well, at least they were sharin' somethin' more than a danged ol' box of popcorn.

BILLY BOB
A true Christian is pure in mind and body.

LU ANN
I wish you'd stop preachin', Billy Bob. Mah Gawd, ever' time we have somethin' important to discuss, you come up with a danged sermon.

BILLY BOB
What in the world are we discussin' that's important?

LU ANN
Your daddy's step-down Hudson Hornet, that's what!

BILLY BOB
My daddy's . . . For cryin' out loud, Lu Ann, sometimes you drive me absolutely nuts!

LU ANN
Well, you don't have to yell, Billy Bob.

BILLY BOB
Ah told you, an' told you, an' told you that we cain't have the Hudson.

LU ANN
Well, why not?

BILLY BOB
'Cause my daddy's got to go over to Big Spring!

LU ANN
Well, it seems plumb funny to me that your daddy picked the very day of the senior picnic to go over to Big Spring. Ah mean, doesn't he know that the senior picnic is jest about the most important event in our whole schoolin' career?

BILLY BOB
Ah don't know if he does or not, he jest . . .

LU ANN
Don't hardly seem fair to look forward to somethin' all these years only to have your daddy come along and mess it up.

BILLY BOB
Daddy ain't messed up nothin', he jest . . .

LU ANN
He's only doin' it for spite, Billy Bob.

BILLY BOB
No, he ain't, he's jest . . .

LU ANN
And spite in my book is jest plain sinful and un-Christian. *(She turns to go.)* Good night, Billy Bob.

BILLY BOB
(Grabbing her arm.) Now wait a minute, Lu Ann. *(They are very close now.)* Oh, boy, uh, uh. Ah will talk to Dad tonight and ask for the car again, okay?

LU ANN
Swell, Billy Bob. *(She kisses him.)* Good night, now.

BILLY BOB
Good night. By gollies, Lu Ann, ah'm gonna make danged sure we git that car.

LU ANN
Fine.

BILLY BOB
Danged sure! *(He exits.)*

(LU ANN watches him for a moment and then enters the house.)

CLAUDINE
(Entering down the stairs, singing.) "Don't let the stars get in your eyes." Well, mah, mah, look who's here. Billy Bob Wortman walk you home?

LU ANN
Yep.

CLAUDINE
Kiss him good night?

LU ANN
Maybe.

CLAUDINE
Well, ah'm glad your daddy never lived to see the day when his only little girl would be standin' on the front porch smoochin' with one of them worthless Wortman boys.

LU ANN
Oh, Ma.

CLAUDINE
'Specially one with green hair.

LU ANN
How do you know? You peeked!

CLAUDINE
Didn't done it! It's all over Bradleyville how them ignernt basketball boys poured green dye or somethin' all over their empty heads.

LU ANN
Pete Honeycutt put 'em up to it.

CLAUDINE
That figgers. All them Honeycutts are crazy. God, ah remember once when Pete's *daddy* and me—oh, well, shoot, never mind. See your brother today?

LU ANN
Naw, he said he was goin' to come over to the school but he never.

CLAUDINE
Yeah, well, ah speck he's off runnin' around some place. Lordy, but he worries me, seems like ever since he come home from Korea he's been rollin' around like a tumbleweed. Foolin' around all day long in Sweetwater or Big Spring and drinkin' all night over to Red Grover's bar. All that drinkin' is no good for him, Lu Ann. If he keeps it up he's gonna wind up in the alcohol ward in the state hospital jest like his cousin Wilbur Bentley, you mark mah words. *(Lights up cigarette.)*

LU ANN
Aw, Ma. Nuthin' like that's gonna happen to Skip.

CLAUDINE

Lord, ah hope not. *(She settles into the armchair.)* Ahh, boy, well now, tell me about the assembly.

LU ANN

Ain't much to tell.

CLAUDINE

Ain't much to tell! Well, if that don't beat all, here you been runnin' around all week talkin' about that-there assembly, and when ah ask you about it, you up and say, "Ain't much to tell."

LU ANN

Oh, gawlee, Ma, it was the same old stuff, dull, dull, dull.

CLAUDINE

Whattayou mean dull, dull, dull?

LU ANN

Oh, you know, first Mr. Palmroy got up and said how the Class of 1953 was one of the best ever at Bradleyville High. Then he had all the teachers stand up and he said how good they were; boy, ah had to laugh at that, but anyway, we gave 'em a big cheer. Then he introduced old Miss Millikan, who's gonna retire this year.

CLAUDINE

Bess Millikan! Retirin'!

LU ANN

Yep, after forty years! Can you imagine?

CLAUDINE

Mah God, Bess Millikan was my English teacher too, twenty-three years ago. Why she musta been a young woman at the time, but even back then we called her "old Miss Millikan."

LU ANN
Well, I cain't imagine her as ever bein' young, gawlee!

CLAUDINE
No, I don't guess anybody ever did. I spoze that's why she was always *Miss* Millikan. I hope you-all had a nice goin'-away for her.

LU ANN
Why, we shore did. Floyd Tatum came out and gave her an orchid.

CLAUDINE
Good.

LU ANN
Then Coach Charlton gave her a letter sweater of her very own to wear to the games.

CLAUDINE
A what?

LU ANN
A letter sweater, with a real Bradleyville letter on the front and a big number 40 on the back. She was gonna give a speech, but she started to cry of course, so we give her a big cheer and she sat down.

CLAUDINE
Why, the poor thing. I feel kinda sorry for her.

LU ANN
Well, I don't see why. Look at all them nice things she got.

CLAUDINE
I know, I know—but even so, it seems—oh, never mind. What happened next?

LU ANN

Then Coach Charlton read off the list of the basketball team and how we almost won district and ever'thing, and then bang, open come the gym doors and here comes the team onto the floor—with green hair! It looked like the Martians had landed or somethin'. Ever'body just hollered and carried on like idiots. We were havin' all kinda fun until stuffy old Mr. Palmroy had us sing the school song and we all went to our classes.

CLAUDINE

Well, it sounds like quite a time.

LU ANN

Uh-huh. But that wasn't the best part. When the noon hour came around, all of us girls that go with the basketball boys pretended that we didn't want to be seen with them.

CLAUDINE

You didn't!

LU ANN

Shore we did. Whenever they'd come around we'd run off. Billy Bob was runnin' after me and fell down into a great old big bunch of tumbleweeds.

CLAUDINE

That figgers.

LU ANN

Pete Honeycutt chased Ruthie Lee Lawell up and down the hall makin' funny noises.

CLAUDINE

Mah, mah, well, you best enjoy yourself while you can, honey, remember that your schoolin' days are the happiest days of your life.

LU ANN
Oh, pooh.

CLAUDINE
Don't "oh, pooh" me, Miss Snippy Face. Ah know what ah'm talkin' about.

LU ANN
Well, if this is the *happiest* time of mah life, ah'm jest not too all fired shore ah want to go on livin'. Gee whiz.

CLAUDINE
You'll eat them words one of these days, believe you me.

LU ANN
What's so doggone happy 'bout dumb old school? I was sittin' there in study hall the other day and I got to lookin' at a picture there on the wall of one of them castles they got over there to Europe and way up in the top part of it was this little tiny door and I got to thinking to myself, boy, what I wouldn't give to git outta here for a spell and go over yonder to where that castle is. Climb up there and open that little door and look out at the trees and gardens and such like and holler out, "Hey, ever'-body, look here, look at me. I've just opened the little door that's at the top of the whole wide world!

CLAUDINE
Well, ah don't know what me and your daddy did wrong in this life to produce such balloon-headed babies. Why weren't you workin' on your lessons 'stead of sittin' there dreamin' up fool notions?

LU ANN
'Cause ah'm sick and tired of school, that's why! Boy, will I be happy to get out of there. Dumb old Mr. Palmroy grouchin' around and dumb old Mrs. Willis in dumb old biology class. "Learnin' the ways and means of the life of the plants

has importance to learnin' the ways of our fellow human creatures." Boy, ah have to laff at that, I tell you.

CLAUDINE
Well, ah don't know . . .

LU ANN
It's dumb.

CLAUDINE
Well, ah don't know . . .

LU ANN
What's a plant got to do with people? Plants jest sit around doin' nuthin'. Gee whiz.

CLAUDINE
Some plants are mighty pretty.

LU ANN
Do you know that there are plants in this world that eat people?

CLAUDINE
Did Mrs. Willis tell you that?

LU ANN
No, she did not. Ah happen to know *that* for a fact.

CLAUDINE
Well, ah don't believe a word of it.

LU ANN
It's the Gawd's truth. Billy Bob and me jest happened to see a picture out to the drive-in that told us all about it.

CLAUDINE
A movin' picture! That's jest all made-up stuff.

LU ANN
This movie jest happened to be based on actual incidents!

CLAUDINE
Oh pooh.

LU ANN
These fellers went plumb up the Amazon River in a great old big canoe jest to find and film these man-eatin' plants.

CLAUDINE
What'd them man-eatin' plants look like?

LU ANN
They had these big red claw-lookin' outfits that grabbed on to you, you see; then there was this clackity, clackity kind of a noise and *gulp,* that's all she wrote.

CLAUDINE
You're makin' this all up.

LU ANN
Ah am not.

CLAUDINE
You are so, too. You and Billy Bob Wortman ain't never seed a movie out to that drive-in in your life.

LU ANN
What are you talkin' about, we go out there most ever' Satti-day night.

CLAUDINE
Not to watch no movie you don't.

LU ANN
Do too!

CLAUDINE
Don't either! You all go out there to smooch and fool around.

LU ANN
Nasty mind.

CLAUDINE
Nothin' nasty 'bout the truth. Ah don't know why they bother to show a movie at all. They oughter jest line up them pickup trucks and turn the *lights* out for a couple of hours.

LU ANN
Lot you know 'bout it.

CLAUDINE
Ah know a lot more than you think. Hangin' around at the drive-in, dreamin' 'bout castles in the air. Honey, you gotta start some serious thinkin' 'bout after you graduate. Now, are you and Ruthie Lee still wantin' to go to that business college in Big Spring?

LU ANN
Business college? My Gawd, Mama, I'm not goin' through all the trouble of gittin' outta one school jest to turn around and walk right into another one.

CLAUDINE
Well, then how 'bout gittin' you that summer job with me at the hospital? It's the best trainin' in the world if you're goin' to go on and be a nurse.

LU ANN
Oh, ah don't know, Mama. Ah don't want to think about it jest yet.

CLAUDINE
Well, you gotta think about it some time.

LU ANN

Ah jest wanna *go,* go anywhere. Outta this house, outta this town, plumb outta the state somewhere.

CLAUDINE

Jest wantin' to go ain't gonna git you anyplace. You gotta plan and work and know where you're goin'.

LU ANN

Ah know, ah know!

CLAUDINE

You know, you know! What do you know?

LU ANN

Ah *know* ah don't want to be stuck all mah life in a little old dried-up West Texas town, emptyin' bedpans at the god-damned hospital, like somebody ah *know!!*

CLAUDINE

(Looks at her a moment, slightly taken aback by the out-burst, then she sighs and slowly shakes her head.) Ah gotta be gittin' on down to work now. Ah got all the fixin's laid out for you in the kitchen. When your brother gits home, you go ahead and cook the supper, will you?

LU ANN

(Very low) Ah'm sorry, Mama.

CLAUDINE

And if you got schoolwork to do, git it done and don't spend the live-long night playin' that durn radio.

LU ANN

Okay, Mama.

CLAUDINE

(Going out the door.) See you later. *(As she exits)* Con-founded kids.

(LU ANN goes straight to the radio and clicks it on. A Western song twangs softly into the room. She starts to dance. The phone rings.)

LU ANN
Comin'. *(She turns down the radio and picks up the receiver.)* Hello . . . Oh, hi, Eveline . . . Nothin', what are you doin'? . . . Chapter 4? Nope, ah haven't read it yet . . . Oh pooh on old Mrs. Willis . . . What? . . . Of course ah'm goin' to the senior picnic . . . You still goin' with Floyd Tatum . . . You-all made up, huh . . . Of course ah'm goin' with Billy Bob, who'd you expect, Milo Crawford? *(She giggles.)* He's got so many blackheads he looks like a pepper shaker . . .

(There is a loud crash outside and we hear SKIP's voice offstage.)

SKIP
Goddamnit to hell!

LU ANN
Ah gotta go now, Eveline, ah think ah hear mah brother comin' in. See you later, kid, 'bye. *(She hangs up the phone, turns off the radio, and hurries into the kitchen just as SKIP stumbles onto the porch. He is followed by DALE LAVERTY. He is dressed in the traditional uniform of West Texas— white shirt, Levi's, cowboy boots, and straw Western hat. DALE LAVERTY is a great, honest, shambling sort of fellow. He wears a rumpled, cheap tan suit.)*

SKIP
Come on in this house, Dale, Goddamnit, come on in. Ma! Lu Ann! Where the hell is ever'body? Sit down, Dale. Ma, where the hell are you?

LU ANN
(Entering from kitchen.) Ma's gone down to work.

SKIP
The devil you say. You gittin' the supper?

LU ANN
Yes, ah am.

SKIP
Then to hell with it. *(To* DALE*)* She couldn't boil a Vyenna
sausage.

LU ANN
Well, so much for you then. *(She turns to go back into the
kitchen.)*

SKIP
Now hold on a minute, damnit. Ah want you to meet
somebody. Dale Laverty, this here is mah little sister,
Lu Ann.

DALE
Howdy.

LU ANN
Hello.

SKIP
Dale drove over from San Angelo to visit me today, ain't that
somethin'. We was in the same outfit in Korea.

LU ANN
Oh, is that right?

SKIP
Damn right, blastin' them gooks. Old Dale was hell on wheels
with a B.A.R., regular John Wayne. Right, Dale?

DALE
Ah never done much really.

SKIP

Never done much! Why, hell's fire, boy, what you talkin'
about? Did you know that this-here boy, he, he, uh, he saved
mah life over there in Korea?

LU ANN

(Interested) Really?

SKIP

Damn right.

DALE

Aw hell, Skip.

SKIP

Saved your brother's butt, that's what he did. Wanna hear
about it?

LU ANN

Lemme turn down the oven and put the salad back in the
icebox first.

SKIP

You go ahead and do that little thing, honey.

(She exits.)

DALE

(Going up to SKIP.*)* Gawlee, Skip, what are you tryin' to do,
ah never saved your life or nuthin'.

SKIP

Shore, shore, I know. So what, we'll jest have some fun with
little sister, okay?

DALE

Well, shore, ah guess.

SKIP

Whattayou think of Lu Ann—nice, huh?

DALE

(Sincerely) She's real pretty.

SKIP

Yes, she is. She's mah one-and-only sister and you are mah one-and-only buddy. Only buddy ah got in the whole lousy world.

DALE

Aw hell, Skip.

SKIP

The only one. You saw how them slobs down at Red's acted. Lived in this lousy town all mah life, served mah stinkin' country in Ko-rea, and they wouldn't even buy me a lousy beer.

DALE

Aw come on, Skip, you know that ain't true.

SKIP

The hell it ain't.

DALE

You got lots of friends in this-here town. What about that-there lodge you joined the other day?

SKIP

The Knights of the White Magnolia? Hell, Dale, none of them fellers are friends of mine. Ah joined that-there lodge to get ahead in this town. Damn right, that lodge is jest a steppin'-stone, buddy. I've got ideas that's gonna put this little old town right on its ear.

DALE

By gollies, Skip, if anybody can do it, you can.

SKIP

You're damn right I can. I got plans, buddy, big plans. Remember Corporal Rosenberg?

DALE

Yeah. Old Four-Eyes, the motor-pool clerk.

SKIP

That's the guy. Well, he had two college degrees. That's right, *two*—an A.M. and a F.M., some damn thing like that. Well, one afternoon when we was havin' some beers over to the N.C.O. club, he told me that even with all his education he wished he had my common sense.

DALE

No kiddin'.

SKIP

That's right. You see, Dale, all them college chumps like Rosenberg is good for is like one thing at a time—you know. But common-sense guys like me can move around, ya see. We can be goin' with three or four deals at once. Hell's fire, ah got me a couple of real-estate ideas figgered out over to Sweetwater that are flat gonna make a bundle.

DALE

Gawlee.

SKIP

Damn right. And that ain't all. After ah talk to old man Cullers over to the bank, and git me a little capital together, ah'm really gonna put 'er in high gear. You see, Dale, I got all these-here opportunities right out in front of me. And ah got the common sense as how to move out and latch hold of 'em.

DALE
Yeah!

SKIP
But you gotta be careful, you know what ah mean?

DALE
Well, ah . . .

SKIP
You just cain't go rushin' straight into things like a damn fool.
No, sir. You gotta move kindly easy-like. Keep your eyes
open and slip around. In business you got to know ever' side
of things affore you decide to pick up the cards.

DALE
Yeah, ah speck so.

SKIP
Did you know that ah wasn't back in this town of Bradleyville more than five minutes affore old Derwood Herring
was over here wantin' me to go in with him in the Western
Auto store?

DALE
Them Western Auto stores is damn-good outfits.

SKIP
Hell, yes, they are!

DALE
We got one over to San Angelo.

SKIP
You know what ah told him? I said, "Now look here, Derwood, I appreciate the hell outta you comin' over here." You
see, Dale, in business matters you always gotta be polite. "But
ah just ain't the kind of feller just to jump on into things this

way. No, sir. Ah gotta put my mind to work on it. Look at
ever' side of this-here deal. Now, you jest come around again,
say, in a month or two, and maybe ah can figger out somethin' for you."

DALE
What did he say to that?

SKIP
What could he say? Hell, Dale, Derwood ain't dumb. He
knows the truth of things. He just sorter mumbled somethin'
like "Well, all right, Skip, if that's how you feel." Then he got
the hell out.

DALE
Did he ever come back?

SKIP
Naw. The back-stabbin' s.o.b. went straight over to Earl Par-
ker's place and got him to go partners.

DALE
That was a damn dirty thing to do.

SKIP
Ah was glad, Dale, glad he done it. Who the hell would want
to spend the rest of their life runnin' a Western Auto store
for Christ's sake?

DALE
Them places ain't much account anyway.

SKIP
Hell, no, they ain't.

DALE
We got one over to San Angelo that ah never liked much.

SKIP

When these real-estate outfits work out, why in ten years or so ah'll not only own that damn Western Auto store but the whole damn block it's sittin' in.

DALE

You'll do 'er too, buddy!

SKIP

You see, Dale, time don't mean a damn thing in the business world. It's what you do with it that counts. How would you like to come over here someday and have old Skip drive you on down to the country club in his new Cadillac, sit around the bar over there with Floyd Kinkaid and all them rich bastards, and talk about oil wells and such like?

DALE

Boy, that would be somethin'.

SKIP

Cain't ever tell, buddy. Why, hell's fire, ah might even buy into that livestock-haulin' outfit you're fixin' to go to work for.

DALE

The Hubbard Brothers?!

SKIP

Hell, yes. Why not? You see, Dale, all ah gotta do is talk to old man Cullers over to the bank and then . . .

LU ANN

(Entering.) All done.

SKIP

Yeah, that's fine, Lu Ann. You see, Dale, all ah need is a little capital, then . . .

LU ANN

What about the story?

SKIP
What story?

DALE
'Bout me savin' your life over to Ko-rea.

SKIP
What the hell you talkin' about?

DALE
You know that time when, uh . . . that story you was gonna
tell Lu Ann there.

SKIP
Oh yeah, well, let's see now. Remember me writin' to you-all
'bout how I was drivin' them convoy trucks over there?

LU ANN
Shore do.

SKIP
Well, sir. There was that time when the Marines caught hell
and was retreatin' from the Chosan reservoir. Remember
readin' that in the newspapers?

LU ANN
Ah think so.

SKIP
Well, we was there! Old Dale and me, a-bringin' them boys
down through the hills. Snow on the ground, cold as hell, and
by God surrounded by the entire Chinese gook army.

LU ANN
Gawlee.

SKIP
Damn right. The hills was covered by them little slant-eyed

bastards like by-God ants! There was five truckloads of us, you see, comin' down this little old dirt road. Cold as hell and dog-assed surrounded. Well, as you can see, we was in some- thin' of a fix, but it looked like we was gonna make it out okay. When all of a sudden they come down on us with their heavy artillery. Wham, wham, wham! In nuthin' flat three of our trucks was nuthin' but smokin' ruin.

LU ANN
Smokin' ruin?

SKIP
That's right, smokin' ruin! Then it happened! Bang, they got me! Direct hit, right on my truck! The next thing I know, ah'm lyin' out in the snow with dead bodies of Marines all around me. Well, sir, ah figgered ah'd best git the hell outta there pronto. So ah got up to take off and that's when ah seed 'em comin'.

LU ANN
Who?

SKIP
Who?! The goddamned gooks, that's who! *(To* DALE*) Who! (Back to* LU ANN*)* About fifty of 'em comin' like a bat out of hell over this little rise and ever' one of 'em comin' right at me, and ah knew, ah *knew* that ah was standin' there a dead man. Nuthin' ah could do but stand there and watch 'em git closer and closer. Then, then by God it happened!

LU ANN
What?

SKIP
Ah heard a noise behind me and here comes old Dale, drivin' with one hand and shootin' with the other. Cuttin' them gooks down like by-God weeds. He tossed down the B.A.R. and, openin' the door of the truck, reached out and picked

me off the ground, threw me into the front seat, and gunned that old truck like Billy Jim hell over the hill and outta there.

LU ANN
Mah gosh.

SKIP
And for doin' that this-here boy was awarded one of the highest medals that this country's got. The Good Conduct Medal with bar.

LU ANN
Wow!

SKIP
Ol' Laverty butt, my best buddy.

DALE
Aw hell, Skip.

SKIP
Yes, sir, that is the man that is sittin' right next to you on the sofa. Old Laverty butt, mah best buddy. *(Suddenly* SKIP *stands up and grasps his stomach.)* Oh God, ah feel it comin' on again.

LU ANN
What's wrong?

SKIP
It's either mah old war wound, or the malaria, or, or—

LU ANN
My God, Skip, what is it?

SKIP
Yes, that's it, ah'm sure that's it.

LU ANN
What?!

SKIP
Oh, gotta go tap this kidney or by God drown.

DALE
Aw hell, Skip. (SKIP *laughs and exits. There is a silence as* DALE *and* LU ANN *grope around for a thread of conversation. With great effort)* So you're a cheerleader, huh?

LU ANN
What?

DALE
Uh—so you're a cheerleader, huh?

LU ANN
Oh, yes.

DALE
That's great.

LU ANN
It's lots of fun.

DALE
Ah'll bet.

(LU ANN *offers tangerine—he declines.)*

LU ANN
You—uh—you play any *ball* over in San Angelo?

DALE
Football. Left tackle, that's on the line.

LU ANN
Yes. Ah know.

DALE
We had a good team. You remember Jack Mathis?

LU ANN
Ah don't think so.

DALE
Well, Jack Mathis was our quarterback and he went over to the A and M and made Honorable Mention All Southwestern Conference Second Team Defensive Guard.

LU ANN
That's neat.

DALE
He's the State Farm insurance man in Big Spring now.

LU ANN
No kiddin'?

DALE
That's right. He's doin' real good. Got him one of them ranch-style homes.

LU ANN
Wow. Uh—whatta*you* gonna do now that your army is over and all that?

DALE
Oh, ah got me a job with the Hubbard Brothers.

LU ANN
(Guessing) Truck drivin'?

DALE
Livestock haulers, West Texas and New Mexico. Ah start next week.

LU ANN
Ah see.

DALE
Because of mah army experience ah got me a rig right away.
Most guys have to start off as a helper but ah got a rig of mah
own right off. Yes, ma'am, big red Mack diesel with air horns
and ever'thing. Boy, it's really somethin'.

LU ANN
Ah'll bet.

DALE
Purrs like a kitten. You wouldn't think an engine that big
could sound so sweet. Boy, it's really somethin', and they give
it to me right off, best old sweetheart in the fleet.

LU ANN
They probably heard about your medal and things.

DALE
(Taken aback) Yeah . . . uh, these your school books?

LU ANN
Biology and history, ugh.

DALE
Boy, ah hated school.

LU ANN
My mama says it's the happiest time of your life. Ever hear
anythin' so silly?

DALE
Ah cain't buy that.

LU ANN
Me neither.

DALE

Whattayou gonna do after you graduate?

LU ANN

Gee, ah don't know. Mama wants me to go on to nursin' school.

DALE

That's a good job for a girl.

LU ANN

Ah spoze.

DALE

Mah sister is a dental assistant.

LU ANN

That's a good job.

DALE

Sure is. She makes pretty good money. Her husband works at Hubbard Brothers too.

LU ANN

Really?

DALE

You bet! They got 'em one of those great old big house trailers.

LU ANN

That's neat.

DALE

Shore is. It's got a livin' room, bathroom, kitchen, the works, and the best thing about it is that if you git tired of bein' in one town you can jest hook 'er up and take off, nuthin' to it. Spoze you were livin' in Snyder or Abilene or somewhere

and you wanted to move to Amarillo? Well, sir, you jest hook
up and take off. Furniture, dishes, clothes, ever'thin', jest
take off. Now that is the way to live!

LU ANN
Gosh yes.

DALE
You pull into one of them trailer parks, you see, an' they got
ever'thang. Gas, water, washin' machines, swings, septic
tanks, some even got swimmin' pools.

LU ANN
Swimmin' pools?

DALE
You bet, and grass and trees and flowers and collie dogs
runnin' around.

LU ANN
Gee, it sounds like heaven.

DALE
Yeah.

(Their eyes meet for a long moment. SKIP *re-enters.)*

SKIP
Whooee, did ah need that!

DALE
(Nervously) You shore were gone a long time.

SKIP
Well, you know how it is, kid. The longer it is, the longer it
takes. You-all gittin' along okay?

DALE

Sure, Skip. Jest fine.

SKIP

Well, now, ain't that real nice. You know, Dale, one of these days old Lu Ann is gonna make some lucky guy one helluva nice wife.

LU ANN

Aw shoot.

SKIP

Whattayou think, old podnah?

DALE

Ah truly believe she will.

SKIP

Damn right. But ah gotta tell you one thing right off. You got competition, boy.

DALE

Ah do?

SKIP

You better believe it. Old Lu Ann's got her a basketball-playin' dude. How many points Billy Bob score agin Snyder, Lu Ann?

LU ANN

Six.

SKIP

You hear that, Dale? Six big ones! God A mighty, what an eye, makes old Bob Cousy look like an amateur.

LU ANN

Billy Bob was doggone good over there to Snyder.

SKIP

Yeah, boy, and a lover too. I hear tell that Lu Ann kissed him so hard the other night that his hair turned as green as alfalfa.

DALE

Sounds like a helluva guy.

SKIP

Damn right! They tell me that when old Billy Bob grows up he's gonna rent his head out to pasture.

LU ANN

(Playfully hitting at him.) Oh, you. Now you quit pickin' on Billy Bob, he's a nice boy.

SKIP

Shore he's a nice *boy*, but maybe it's about time you started thinkin' about a nice *man*. An adult, grown-up man, 'stead of some pimply-faced, nose-pickin' kid. Somebody that can shake them bed springs till your toes curl up and your teeth rattle.

LU ANN

(Holding her hands over her ears.) Ah ain't gonna listen no more.

SKIP

Listen to what? Hell, ah never said nuthin'. Hey, Dale, you remember them wooden beds they had in that whorehouse in Tokyo?

DALE

(Embarrassed and uncomfortable) No, Skip, ah, uh, don't, uh, remember.

LU ANN

Ah wish you wouldn't always talk dirty thataway.

SKIP

Who's talkin' dirty? Them wooden beds is a by-God historical fact. We was talkin' about 'em over to mah lodge meetin' the other night, Dale, and old L. D. Alexander said . . .

LU ANN

Boy, that figgers. Bunch of dirty-minded old men.

SKIP

What do you mean, "dirty-minded old men"? It jest so happens that some of the most important men in this town are members of the Knights of the White Magnolia.

LU ANN

That ain't the way ah heard it.

SKIP

What ain't the way you heard it? It's the by-God truth. Ain't that right, Dale?

DALE

Well, gawlee, Skip, ah don't know.

SKIP

(To LU ANN*)* You see there?

LU ANN

Sara Beth Phelps was over here the other day and told Mama that she didn't like for Rufe to go to them meetin's 'cause nobody does nuthin' but drink whiskey, play dominoes, and git into big fights.

SKIP

Well, what in the name of Jesus H. Christ does Sara Beth Phelps know anyway!

LU ANN

Rufe Phelps is a member, ain't he?

SKIP

Shore he's a member. That's why Sara Beth don't know a
damn thing. 'Cause members ain't spozed to tell nobody,
wives, or nuthin', what goes on in our meetin's.

LU ANN

How's come?

SKIP

How's come? 'Cause it's secret, that's how's come! We do lots
of secret important things.

LU ANN

Shore, shore, like talkin' about wooden beds in Tokyo whore-
houses.

SKIP

That was before the meetin', damnit, before the secret stuff.
And who the hell ever taught you to say whorehouse! You
tryin' to shame the family in front of company?

DALE

Ah, hell, Skip.

LU ANN

You jest said it yourself not two seconds ago.

SKIP

That don't mean you gotta go repeatin' it all over town. How
about that, Dale? A little old fatty-legged high-school girl
goin' around sayin' dirty words in her own by-God house. Ah
don't know what the goddamned world's comin' to.

LU ANN

Pickin' on me ain't gonna change a thing. Ever'body in town
knows that that-there lodge ain't worth a hill of beans and
you're just puttin' a lot of stock into somethin' that ain't
nuthin' at all.

DALE
(Getting up.) Well, ah speck ah better . . .

SKIP
That lodge is jest a steppin'stone, a steppin'stone, that's all!

LU ANN
Uh-huh. *(She mimes crossing a stream.)* Step, step, kerplunk!

SKIP
Come on, Dale, let's git the hell out of here and go on back
to Red's place!

DALE
Well, uh, shore . . .

LU ANN
Mama says, if you keep hangin' out over to Red's place,
you're gonna wind up bein' just like Wilbur Bentley.

SKIP
Well, ah don't give a damn if ah do. At least in the alcohol
ward ah won't be pestered to death by a big-mouthed little
sister. Now come on, Dale, let's go!

DALE
You go ahead, Skip! Ah'll be right with you.

SKIP
(Exiting.) Pick on a feller's lodge. Might as well pick on his
country or his flag or somethin'. No damn respect, that's the
trouble. No by-God respect. *(He exits.)*

(There is a moment of silence.)

DALE
Old Skip's a lotta fun, ain't he?

LU ANN
Sometimes.

DALE
Lot of that stuff he said earlier he didn't really mean.

LU ANN
Oh, well, ah don't reckin it matters.

DALE
Listen, do you think it would be okay if ah called you some time? Ah mean, uh, you and that feller of yours ain't engaged or nuthin', are you?

LU ANN
Oh, shoot, no, we jest kinda go with each other, you know.

DALE
Shore. Well then, would it be okay?

LU ANN
What?

DALE
If ah maybe could call you or somethin'?

LU ANN
Oh, sure, Dale, that would be real neat.

DALE
Okay, by golly, ah'll jest do that. Real soon.

LU ANN
Swell.

DALE
Well, uh, so long.

LU ANN

So long. See you soon. *(DALE exits. She watches after him for a moment and then crosses into the room. She stands for a moment at the radio.)* Dale Laverty—Dale Laverty, gee, that's a pretty name. *(She switches on the radio; Western music booms forth as the act ends.)*

ACT II

The act takes place in 1963 in Red Grover's bar. A small, dim, beer-smelling West Texas dive. Lots of beer advertisements on the wall. Coors, Lone Star, Pearl, Miller's, etc. A small wooden bar, couple of tables and chairs. A beat-up jukebox. Above the bar is a large sign: WE RESERVE THE RIGHT TO REFUSE SERVICE TO ANYONE. RED'*s place has seen a lot of beer-swilling, head-knocking, gut-rumbling life and looks it.*

As the scene opens we find RED GROVER *standing behind the bar, glumly watching* RUFE PHELPS *and* OLIN POTTS *play checkers.*

RUFE

Watch out there, watch out what you're doin' there!

OLIN

Hell, Rufe, it's mah move.

RUFE

Ah know it's your blamed move. But you cain't move mah checkers. Only yours.

OLIN

Ah ain't movin' yours, only ones ah'm movin' is the black uns.

RUFE

Your finger touched that checker right there and that checker is by God red.

OLIN

Mah finger never touched nuthin'. All ah'm movin' is the black uns.

RUFE

Red seen it. Hey, Red, didn't he touch this-here checker?

RED

Who gives a damn.

OLIN

Ah never touched nuthin'!

RUFE

Did so too!

OLIN

Didn't never either!

RUFE

Done it!

OLIN

Didn't!

RED

For Christ's sake! If you two cain't play that damned game without fightin' about it, then you can by God get the hell outta here.

RUFE

Well, hell, Red, he cheated.

OLIN

Ah never neither.

RED
(Quietly) Ah ain't gonna tell you two again.

RUFE
Ah'm tired of playin' anyway.

OLIN
That's 'cause you're losin'.

RUFE
Shore ah'm losin'. How can anybody win with you a-movin' any damn checker on the board that pleases you?

OLIN
Ah'm only movin' the black uns!

RUFE
Ah never seen nuthin' like you, Olin Potts! Cheat at horseshoes, cheat at checkers, cheat at dominoes, cheat at ever'thang!

OLIN
Ah never cheat at nuthin'! And you know it!

RUFE
Never cheat? How 'bout the last time we went bowlin'. Hey, Red, he knocked down the by-God pin boy and called it a spare.

OLIN
Well, hell, ah figgered he should count for somethin'; 'sides that, a movin' target's harder to hit.

RUFE
(To RED*)* You see there.

RED
Boy, you two are somethin' else. Anybody want another beer?

RUFE
Naw. Ah'm already gittin' the bloats.

RED
How about you, Olin?

OLIN
Two's mah limit, Red.

RED
(Mimicking) "Two's mah limit, Red." Some customers. Sit around here all day long and buy four lousy beers.

RUFE
Ah cain't help it if beer bloats me.

RED
Well, damnit, drink somethin' else!

RUFE
Ah don't like nuthin' else.

RED
Oh, for Christ's sake.

RUFE
What are you-all so all-fired peckish about, Red? Me and Olin never drink more than four beers, ain't that right, Olin?

OLIN
Two's mah limit.

RED
Jesus Christ, some business ah got here. Bloated checker players all day long and by-God drunken maniacs at night.

RUFE
You're talkin' about Skip Hampton, ain't you?

OLIN
What's old Skip done now?

RUFE
Didn't you hear about what he did?

OLIN
Hell no, ah never hear about nuthin'.

RED
Stupid bastard tried to kill himself in here last night.

OLIN
Kill himself!

RED
That's right.

RUFE
Had him a knife, didn't he?

RED
Hell, no. The crazy son-of-a-bitch cut his throat with a broken bottle.

OLIN
Cut his throat! Well, whattayou know about that.

RED
Damnedest thing ah ever saw in mah life.

OLIN
What the hell happened?

RED
He came in here about, oh, 2:30 or 3:00 yesterday afternoon, lookin' like hell as usual, and started chuggin' down the old Thunderbird wine. Come about 8:00 he's drunk as billy hell and starts to mouth off again about Ko-rea.

OLIN
Oh, God, not again.

RED
That's right, them same old sad-assed stories. Well, sir, Pete Honeycutt was standin' here at the bar and he turns over to Skip and says, "Why don't you shove it, Hampton—nobody wants to hear that old crap any more— Hell, that damned war's been over for *ten years.*"

OLIN
What did he do then?

RED
Well, sir, old Skip looks up and says, "You're a goddamned liar." That's right, jest as cool as you please. "You're a god-damned liar."

OLIN
Skip said that to Pete Honeycutt. My God, what did Pete do?

RED
Hell, you know old Pete Honeycutt, nobody calls him a liar. The next thing I know he's got Skip by the shirt front and slammed up into the corner. "Listen, you sad sack of crap," he says, "this is nineteen and goddamned sixty-three—you ain't no Korean hero no more—you're nuthin' but a stinkin' wino bum, the goddamned town joke!" Then he spins him around and kicks him in the ass. Knocked him right up agin the bar here.

RUFE
God Almighty.

RED
Well, sir, Skip gits up real slow like and ah figger he's gonna tangle with old Pete.

OLIN
Did he?

RED
Hell, no. He jest stood there lookin' at Pete for a second and then he started to cry.

RUFE
He did what?

RED
He started bawlin'. Damnedest thing ah ever seen. Stood there like a damned fool and cried like a baby.

OLIN
Whattayou know about that.

RED
Hell, ah liked to died laughin'. The whole place nearly come apart, old Pete jest doubled up and hollered. Jesus, it was funny! Then, by God, while we was laughin' there at him he reached behind him, got this-here beer bottle, broke it on the bar, and pulled the edge across his throat.

RUFE
My God!

RED
Hell, ah thought he was sure-enough dead. Ah mean, the blood jumped clean across the room. It's a damn good thing old Doc Crowley was across the street there to the Dixie Dinette or Skip would be on a slab at Strong's Funeral Home 'stead of the hospital. By God I've seen some pretty wild things in this dump, but last night takes the blue goddamned ribbon. Ah was moppin' up blood and broken glass for an hour.

OLIN
By gollies, ah don't know. It seems to me that ever since our lodge broke up, old Skip's jest sorter gone on downhill.

RED

That's bullshit! Skip Hampton was born goin' downhill, that stinkin' little lush is nuthin' but a washout and a loser.

RUFE

You know the one ah feel sorry for is his mother.

OLIN

Damn right, it's a shame that a fine woman like Claudine Hampton has got a burden like that on her.

RUFE

Two burdens, you're forgittin' about Lu Ann.

RED

Lu Ann, now there's a hot little number for you. *(He chuckles.)* Tough as a damned boot.

RUFE

That girl's plum wild now, that's a by-God fact.

OLIN

Well, ah don't know.

RUFE

You don't know! Why, hell, Olin, she's been movin' through this town like a tornado ever since she got shed of that husband of hers four or five years ago and moved back from over there to Snyder.

OLIN

Well, ah know all that, but hell, Rufe, she jest blows off a little steam now and again. She ain't *bad* or nuthin' like that.

RUFE

Any woman that would sit around a bar like this-here one drinkin' beer and smokin' cigarettes with a bunch of old hard-headed men is by God down in mah book as *bad!*

RED
Now hold on there, you're talkin' about some of my best customers.

OLIN
By God, Rufe, you got you a plum narrow mind, ah'll be damned if you don't—

RUFE
Now jest what the hell do you mean by that!

RED
He's tryin' to tell you that you're skinny-brained, Rufe.

RUFE
Who's skinny-brained?

OLIN
You are, that's who, you got a skinny brain in a big fat head!

RED
(Laughing) That's tellin' him, Olin.

RUFE
(Leaping up.) By God, Olin, now you've gone too damn far. *(He assumes an old-time fighting stance.)* Git up, git up, so's ah can knock you down.

RED
Attaboy, Rufe!

OLIN
Don't be a damned fool, Rufe, sit down and forgit it.

RUFE
Ah damned well won't forgit it. Now, by God, Olin, git up and fight.

RED
Go ahead, Olin, you can take him.

(The door opens and LU ANN *enters. The years have hardened
her prettiness into a tough, smooth gloss. Her figure is still
excellent. She is drugstore pretty, cologne and lipstick pretty.
She wears the white uniform of a beauty operator.)*

LU ANN
What the hell's goin' on in here?

RED
Come on in, Lu Ann, you're jest in time for the fight of the
century. We got old Hurricane Skinny-Brain versus Two's-
My-Limit Lewis.

LU ANN
My God, what are you and Olin fightin' about now, Rufe?

RUFE
Well, we, ah, er . . .

RED
Go ahead, Rufe, tell her.

OLIN
We was jest arguin' about a bowlin' score, Lu Ann, that's
all.

LU ANN
Ah heard about you sports over to the Bradleyville Bowl. Still
smackin' down the pin boys there, Olin?

OLIN
Got two last Wednesday.

LU ANN
Damn good goin'.

RUFE

You ought to see 'em jump around when old Olin gits up there—it's plumb comical.

LU ANN

Sounds like it. My gawd, Red, gimme a beer before ah flat dry up and die.

RED

Comin' up, Lu Ann! Whattayou doin' over here today? You and Maud Lowery have another fight?

LU ANN

Aw, that goddamned old bag! What she knows about bein' a beautician wouldn't stuff a horny toad's butt.

RED

Better watch your step, Lu Ann, or Maud's gonna fire you one of these days.

LU ANN

Fire me! That'll be the goddamn day. Maud Lowery's Bon-Ton Beauty *Saloon*, for Christ's sake. There ain't a woman in this town comes into that shop wantin' anyone else to do their hair but me. Maud Lowery gits her hands on you and you walk out lookin' like a gunny sack. She couldn't curry a coyote and she's got the sand to call herself a beautician! Hell, ah studied beauty operation, Red, you know that. Probably could have had a shop of my own by now if it weren't for that worthless Dale Laverty.

OLIN

Where is old Dale now?

LU ANN

Who gives a damn. Why, I never hear from him any more, not since he pulled out on me one fine night with a gut full of hootch and snakes in his boots. Left me to bring up little Charmaine all by mahself.

RUFE
You're livin' with your ma now, ain't you, Lu Ann?

LU ANN
Yep, same old place. Mama helps me take care of Charmaine.
She only works part time over to the hospital now.

RED
Been over to see your brother today?

LU ANN
Sure, sure, ah seen him.

OLIN
How's he gittin' along?

LU ANN
Well, Doc Crowley says he's goin' to be okay but ah don't
know, he sure look peekity to me. Boy howdy, what a damn-
fool thing to do.

OLIN
Well, he'd had a lot to drink, ah spoze.

LU ANN
Skip always has a lot to drink. Maybe this will slow him down
for a little while.

OLIN
(Getting up.) Well, ah gotta be gettin' back to the farm.
Chores to do. *(To* RUFE*)* You still wanna set that trotline in
the mornin'?

RUFE
Hell, yes, I wanna set that line. I found a place out there on
the lake that jest smells catfishy. Pick me up at the house
about 4:30, okay?

OLIN
Will do. Well, ah'll see you-all later. *(He exits.)*

RUFE
So long, Olin.

LU ANN
You still workin' over to the refinery, Rufe?

RUFE
You bet. Same old job.

LU ANN
How's Sara Beth gittin' along these days?

RUFE
Well, she had the misery in her shoulder again last winter, but other than that she's all right, ah guess.

(The door opens and CORKY OBERLANDER *enters.* CORKY *is an open, friendly-type fellow in his mid-thirties. He wears khaki work clothes and a baseball cap.)*

CORKY
Howdy, Rufe.

RUFE
Hey there, Corky.

RED
Hey, Corky—whattayou say, boy?

CORKY
Don't say it, Red. How 'bout a beer?

RED
Comin' up.

CORKY
(Spotting LU ANN.*)* Well, hello there, pretty girl. Hey, Red, who in the world is this pretty little thing?

RED
Lu Ann Laverty, Corky Oberlander.

CORKY
Well, I'm happy to meet you, Lu Ann Laverty.

LU ANN
Well, I'm happy to meet you, Corky Overlander.

RED
Corky here is an inspector with the Highway Department.

CORKY
Yep, got transferred over here from Abilene. Didn't think I was going to like it much till now.

LU ANN
Aw hell.

CORKY
Care to join me at a table?

LU ANN
Suits me.

RUFE
Well, ah gotta be goin'.

RED
Take it easy, Rufe.

RUFE
If I'm late for supper, old Sara Beth will be mad as hell. *(He exits.)*

RED
You two want anythin' else?

CORKY
Nuthin' for me, thanks. *(To* LU ANN*)* How about you?

LU ANN
Naw, ah'm okay.

RED
That figgers. I'm gonna go out back and stack some cases. If anybody comes in, sing out for me, will you?

CORKY
Will do. *(*RED *exits. There is a long pause.)* Well, here we are.

LU ANN
Looks like.

CORKY
Want me to play the jukebox?

LU ANN
Naw, sometimes them damn twangy guitars git into my nose.

CORKY
Yeah, well. How come the white uniform—you a nurse or somethin'?

LU ANN
Nurse? Hell no, ah'm a beauty technician.

CORKY
No kiddin'.

LU ANN
That's right. Ah got me a diploma from the Sanford School of Beauty Culture over there in San Angelo.

CORKY
Well now, that's real fine.

LU ANN
Sure is. Ah went to night school, took me twelve whole months.

CORKY
Twelve months?

LU ANN
That's right. I probably could have finished a whole lot sooner if it weren't for that worthless Dale Laverty.

CORKY
Your husband?

LU ANN
Mah *ex*-husband. Ah'm divorced.

CORKY
Ah see.

LU ANN
You married?

CORKY
Ah was once.

LU ANN
What happened?

CORKY
Oh, ah don't know, Peggy Sue and ah jest never seemed to git along. Seemed like ever' time I was fixin' to move in, she was fixin' to move out. Never could get it together.

LU ANN

Boy, ah know what you mean there, buddy. With me and
Dale it was trucks and trailer houses! You ever live in a
goddamned trailer house?

CORKY

Nope.

LU ANN

Boy, you ain't missed nuthin'. Cramped, miserable little old
tin-boxie outfits—burn up all summer and freeze off all winter. No room to do a damned thing in. Dale would blow a fart
and my eyes would water for three days.

CORKY

Sounds like a helluva home life.

LU ANN

Oh, man, it was de-loox. Stay out at them damned trailer
parks, might as well live on a tumbleweed farm. Two or three
burnt-up little old trees, a couple of splintery teeter-totters,
and five hundred rattlesnakes.

CORKY

Rattlesnakes?

LU ANN

You bet your life, *rattlesnakes!* Hell, they used to crawl up
under that goddamned trailer house like they owned it.

CORKY

Jesus!

LU ANN

You said it, pal.

CORKY

Why the hell didn't you move into a real house?

LU ANN

Old Dale said he didn't want to be tied down. "Wanna be movin' around," he said, "free as a bird." Boy, there's a laugh for you. We moved from San Angelo to Snyder and that was it. That trailer sat in the Shady Grove Mobile Home Park until the tires rotted off. Hell's fire, that was no way to live. 'Specially after Charmaine come along.

CORKY

Charmaine?

LU ANN

Mah little *girl.* Ah didn't tell you ah had a little girl, did ah?

CORKY

No.

LU ANN

Well, she's just the prettiest little thang around, that's all. Good as gold, never no noise or trouble, no, sir, not even when she was a baby. Didn't even cry at night.

CORKY

Whattayou know.

LU ANN

Well, anyways, here ah was stuck out at the Shady Grove in Snyder with a little baby girl to look after and nuthin' to do all day but hunt rattlesnakes with an O'Cedar mop.

CORKY

What was Dale doin' all this time?

LU ANN

Dale! Hell, he was always off deliverin' cattle for the god-damn Hubbard Brothers. Be gone weeks at a time in that damn truck of his. Then when he was home that's all he could talk about. Trucks. God, ah got sick of it. Kenworth,

Mack, Reo, White, GMC, International, hell, you'd think they was Presidents of the United States or somethin'. I never went nowhere and he'd come home and gas about all the places he'd been. So one boozy evenin' when he was home lappin' up the Jim Beam and talkin' about the new shower baths at the Top of the World truck stop in Moriarty, New Mexico, ah went right through the roof. "Listen, you flap-mouthed son-of-a-bitch," ah said, "if that cattleshit-smellin' semi you got out in the yard there means more to you than me and li'l Charmaine, why don't you jest haul your butt into the cab and boom on outta here for good."

CORKY
What happened?

LU ANN
He did it! Slammed out of the trailer, ground about fourteen gears, knocked over the mailbox, ran over our mangy collie dog, and took off down the road. Never saw him again—he didn't even show up at the divorce trial.

CORKY
So you come on back here, huh?

LU ANN
Yep. Buried the dog, sold the trailer, picked up Charmaine, and come on home to Bradleyville.

CORKY
That's a damn shame.

LU ANN
What is?

CORKY
Your marriage breakin' up and all that.

LU ANN
Oh, hell, nuthin' to trouble yourself about. Ah think it was
probably for the best.

CORKY
Think so?

LU ANN
Sure. Ah'm doin' okay. Got a good job over to the beauty
shop, drink a few beers now and then, watch the television,
you know.

CORKY
Shore, shore. Ever git the itch to go on any moonlight truck
rides?

LU ANN
Long or short haul?

CORKY
Either way you want.

LU ANN
No, thanks. From now on, ah go by automobile or not at all.

CORKY
You're an automobile goer, are you?

LU ANN
Sometimes. What kinda car you got?

CORKY
Chivy.

LU ANN
What year?

CORKY
Bran'-new Impala.

LU ANN
Good model. Hey, remember when they had them step-down Hudson Hornets?

CORKY
Shore do.

LU ANN
There was a helluva car. The fella ah went with in high school had one of them. Boy, we went ever'where in that thang. Step down and saddle up.

CORKY
Lots of leg room, huh?

LU ANN
It was a damn-good car. Went to the senior picnic in that car. Jesus, you shoulda seen ever'body's head turn.

CORKY
Big day, huh?

LU ANN
The best. Gawd, ah'll never forget it. Me and the captain of the basketball team in a great old big shiny Hudson. Hot damn!

CORKY
Well, ah never owned no Hudson, but ah did have me a Kaiser once.

LU ANN
A Kaiser!

CORKY
A Kaiser. A great old big Kaiser with a silver buffalo-head hood ornament.

LU ANN
God, them was ugly cars.

CORKY
Ugliest cars in the world. They ain't never made anythin' bigger and uglier than my old green Kaiser. Hell, ah bet that damn thing weighed five ton, got about two miles to the gallon, and burned more oil than the *Super Chief*. I had a wreck in that damn thing once—hit an Oldsmobile head-on.

LUANN
What happened?

CORKY
Totaled that damned Olds, tore it to pieces. Put the block right in the back seat, and that Kaiser? One broken headlight. That's right, one broken headlight! That Olds was totaled and the Kaiser only had a broken headlight. That car was by Gawd built. Solid, you know.

LU ANN
They built 'em good back then.

CORKY
Damn right they did. A buddy of mine nearly killed me with that car one time.

LU ANN
How come?

CORKY
Well, we was goin' deer huntin' one year, me and a bunch of guys. Couple of us took a pickup and loaded ever'thin' in the back—the tent, the bedrolls, the rifles, some boxes of chow, all that crap, and took off, with the rest of the guys followin' in my Kaiser. Well, sir, we was movin' on down the road drinkin' six-packs of Pearl and generally jackassin' around when old Len Hanawald, who was drivin' my Kaiser,

decided he'd race us. Hell, that car wouldn't do more than sixty goin' straight downhill, but old Len hit the horn and around us he comes. Well, sir, ah leadfooted that pickup and take him like he's standin' still—about a quarter of a mile down the road ah come to this intersection with a great old big stop sign lookin' right at me. So bein' a good citizen, ah screech to a halt. Ah no sooner get stopped when somethin' makes me look into the rear-view mirror and all ah can see is this silver buffalo comin' right at me. Ah mean, the whole rear-view mirror is nuthin' but a big silver buffalo. Next thing ah know, Len has piled into the back of the pickup at sixty fat miles an hour. Hell, we scattered bedrolls, .30–30's, and Campbell's pork and beans all over West Texas. Put mah head smooth through the windshield. Sixteen stitches.

LU ANN
Jeeezus!

CORKY
Knocked out all mah front teeth. These are false. Look real, don't they?

LU ANN
Shore do. Whatever happened to that car?

CORKY
The Kaiser? Oh, ah gave it to mah brother when ah went into the army and he tore it up some way.

LU ANN
That's a damn shame. You got a dime?

CORKY
Yeah. *(He gives her a dime, she plays the jukebox. Song comes on low.)*

LU ANN
Ah got a brother that's pretty good at tearin' up things too.

CORKY
Cars?

LU ANN
Lives.

CORKY
Lives!

LU ANN
That's right, pal, lives! His life, mah life, our mama's life. You recollect that king that ever'thin' he touched turned to gold?

CORKY
King Midas?

LU ANN
That's the dude. Well, mah brother, Skip, has a touch too, only ever'thin' he touches goes bad. Cain't hold no job, on the goddamn bum all the time, livin' off my mama like a leech. Now he's flat on his can in the hospital with a cut throat.

CORKY
Was that your brother that did that?

LU ANN
That's the fella. Old playboy Skip. Anythin' for a laugh.

CORKY
Ah've never heard of such a thing. Cuttin' his own throat! Jesus, that makes me goose-pimply jest thinkin' about it. What's wrong with him, is he crazy or somethin'?

LU ANN
No. No, ah don't think Skip's crazy, he jest cain't seem to catch hold of anything, that's all—never seemed to get started. Never married, never held on to a job very long. Jest sorter hung around year after year boozin' it up and dreamin' up big plans.

CORKY
What kind of plans?

LU ANN
Oh, all kinds of plans. Catfish farmin', aluminum siding, uranium prospectin', real estate, anythin' that would make a quick buck. Hell's fire, he even went into the chinchilla business.

CORKY
Oh, good God.

LU ANN
Was gonna make a fortune. Built a bunch of cages in the storeroom and bought him some chinchillas. Nuthin' to it, he says. Feed 'em a little alfalfa and let 'em breed away.

CORKY
Sounds easy enough.

LU ANN
Oh, hell yes! He had 'em about a month when the first norther blew in. 'Course Skip was off drunk somewhere and didn't plug in the 'lectric heater he had in there to keep 'em warm, so they all froze. Poor little old things all humped up in them wire cages froze stiff. Skip came back home and tried to skin 'em, but it was too late then.

CORKY
What kinda work does your brother do now?

LU ANN
Pumps gas over to the Texaco station when he's sober. Aw, to hell with him. Tell me some more about yourself.

CORKY
Well, ah was over to . . .

(The door opens and MILO CRAWFORD *makes a furtive entrance. He glances nervously around.)*

MILO
Hello.

CORKY
Howdy.

LU ANN
Well, ah'll be damned. If it ain't old Milo Crawford.

MILO
Hello. Is, uh, is Red around any place?

CORKY
He's out back. *(Calling out)* Hey, Red, you got a customer.

RED
(From offstage) Tell him to keep his shirt on for a minute, damnit!

MILO
(Very low) No hurry, Red.

LU ANN
Well, how you been there, Milo?

MILO
Oh, fine, jest fine.

LU ANN
Good.

(There is a long pause while MILO *bumbles around.)*

MILO
Ah beg your pardon, miss, but do ah know you?

LU ANN
Why, of course you do, Milo. My Gawd, we went to high school together.

MILO
Oh, ah see. *(He doesn't.)*

LU ANN
Ah was Lu Ann Hampton.

MILO
You mean you ain't any more?

LU ANN
Well, no, Milo, ah got married. Mah name is Laverty now.

MILO
Oh, ah see. *(He goes up to* CORKY.*)* Is this Mr. Laverty?

CORKY
Mr. Laverty?!

LU ANN
Good God, Milo, git your head back in the socket! You still don't know me, do you?

MILO
Well, to tell the truth, no, ma'am, ah don't. But Mr. Laverty here looks kindly familiar.

CORKY
Goddamnit, ah ain't Mr. Laverty!

LU ANN
For Christ's sake, Milo, you ain't got the sense God gave a tumblebug.

RED

(Entering.) What can ah do for you . . . *(He spots* MILO.*)* What in the name of hell!

MILO

(Grinning and fawning around.) Howdy there, Red.

RED

Whattayou doin' in here, Milo, the church burn down or somethin'?

MILO

No, ah, nuthin' like that, Red.

RED

Uh-huh. You know, Milo, if your mama knew that you was in here, she'd flat bust a gusset. She ain't dropped dead or nuthin' like that, has she?

MILO

Oh no, Mama is in real fine health, thank you.

RED

Well, was there anythin' you wanted?

MILO

Oh, ah don't know. Let's see, uh, Miller, Schlitz, Bud, Pearl, uh-huh. All them is kinds of beer, ain't they?

RED

That's right, Milo.

MILO

Ah see. You don't sell Dr. Pepper, do you?

RED

No, Milo, we don't.

MILO
Well, then, uh, how about a pack of them potato chips?

RED
Comin' right up, Milo. That'll be fifteen cents.

MILO
They're only a dime over to the drugstore.

RED
Well, this ain't the goddamned drugstore! Now, do you want
'em or not?

MILO
Yes, sir.

RED
Well?

MILO
Well, what?

RED
Milo, don't tell me you have defied God, your mama, and the
First Baptist Church to come in here and buy a damned pack
of potato chips. Now what the hell else do you want?

MILO
Oh, ah come over here to see if you-all wanted to contribute
to the Jaycees' Beautify Bradleyville Campaign.

RED
You're a Jaycee nowadays, are you, Milo?

MILO
Yes, sir, and ah am on the committee to visit the store owners
and git them to make a contribution so's we can beautify
Bradleyville.

LU ANN

You the same bunch of fellas that put the statue of Colonel
Kinkaid in the city park?

MILO

(With great pride) Yes, ma'am, that was us all right.

LU ANN

Ugliest damn thing ah ever saw in mah life.

RED

That damned statue is so ugly even the pigeons won't shit on
it. What the hell you monkey nuts got in mind for beautiful
this year, Milo?

MILO

The, uh, money goes to repair the cemetery wall.

RED

Oh, it does, does it.

MILO

Yes, the old one is a disgrace to the community. It's full of
cracks and splotches and spidery things.

RED

Well, now ain't that a goddamned shame.

MILO

Yes, it is. *(He pulls out a small notebook.)* Now, what can ah
put you down for?

RED
Nuthin'.

MILO
Nuthin'?

RED

That's right, pal, nuthin'. N-U-T-H-I-N. As far as ah'm concerned, that splotchy, cracked, old spidery wall is damned
fine with me. It's got by God character. Lots more character
than this damn town has. Bradleyville. Jesus, how ah ever
wound up in this burnt-out collection of cowboys and tumbleweeds is beyond me. For two cents ah'd sell this damn
dump and haul ass back to Meridian, Mississippi, where ah by
God belong.

MILO

We'd sure hate to see you go, Red.

RED

Oh, hell, yes, you would. You and your mama and the rest of
the damn Baptists would hold a regular wake if ah left,
wouldn't you? Have a damn parade most likely, with all the
goody-goodies on one side of the street and all the booze-
soaked, beer-swillin', fat-gutted winos on the other. After
ah'm gone, you-all can put up another statue in that patch of
dirt you call a city park, make it even uglier than the one of
that senile, old idiot Colonel Kinkaid. And on the base you
can put this-here inscription, *Red Grover, he hated ever' minute of it.* Now, get on outta here, Milo. Ah'm tired of lookin'
at you.

MILO

Well, gawlee, Red, ah . . .

RED

Now wait a minute, Milo. Come to think of it, there is somethin' you can do for me.

MILO

Why sure, Red. Ah'd be happy to do anythin' ah can.

RED

Well, sir, you go on back down to that Jaycee meetin' and tell them goddamned deadbeats to git over here and pay their goddamn beer tabs, and ah'll give you enough money to put up a splotchy wall plumb around the whole town of Bradley-ville.

MILO

Well, that, uh . . . we, uh . . . they . . .

RED

Now git your ass outta here. Ah got work to do!

MILO

Ah'm goin', ah'm goin'. Ah guess ah better be goin'. It sure was nice to meet you, uh, Mr. and Mrs., uh . . .

CORKY

If you say *Laverty* ah'm gonna belt you!

MILO

Well, uh, no . . . Ah mean . . .

RED

Git outta here!

MILO

Well, it's shore been nice. *(Crosses back for potato chips.)*

RED

Git!

(MILO exits in a hurry.)

LU ANN

(Laughing) Old Milo Crawford, by God, he ain't changed in ten years.

RED

(Muttering) Bloated checker players, drunken maniacs, and by-God, bumble-dickin' Jaycees. *(He exits.)*

CORKY

Jest exactly what the hell was that, anyway?

LU ANN

That was a Milo Crawford.

CORKY

You got any more like that around this town?

LU ANN

Naw, old Milo's one of a kind, thank God.

CORKY

Oh, ah don't know. Mah boss over to Abilene would have run him a close second.

LU ANN

Is that a fact?

CORKY

Damn right. God, was ah happy to transfer out of there.

LU ANN

How long you been with the highway?

CORKY

'Bout eight years.

LU ANN

Red says you're an inspector. What do you inspect?

CORKY

Dirt.

LU ANN

What kinda dirt?

CORKY
The kinda dirt they put on the highway affore they shoot asphalt all over it.

LU ANN
Uh-huh. What else?

CORKY
What else what?

LU ANN
What else do you do?

CORKY
That's it.

LU ANN
Just go around lookin' at dirt?

CORKY
What's wrong with that?

LU ANN
Well, I don't know, it jest seems kindly piddlin'.

CORKY
What do you mean, piddlin'? It's a damned important job.

LU ANN
What's so damned important about lookin' at dirt?

CORKY
(Patiently) If the grade of fill underneath the asphalt isn't right, you get holes in the highway, that's what's so damned important about dirt.

LU ANN
Well, you must be doin' a pretty piss-poor job. Ever' god-

damned highway in this state is as holey as Billy Graham's mother-in-law.

CORKY

Well, goddamn! What the hell do you know about anythin'. Goddamn beauty operator.

LU ANN

Beauty *technician*, you dumb, dirt-lookin' gourd-head!

CORKY

Dirt-lookin' gourd-head! By God, woman, you can git plumb nasty sometimes.

LU ANN

My mama once told me there was nuthin' nasty about the truth.

CORKY

Oh yeah? Your mama ever say anythin' about sittin' around beer bars and pickin' up strangers!

LU ANN

Pickin' up strangers! Ah'm not the one that walked in here and said, "Why, looky here, Red, who in the world is this pretty little thing?" Hell, that-there line went out with the by-God *zoot suit.*

CORKY

Yeah, well, ah guess ah jest ain't as up to date as the rest of your boyfriends in this dump.

LU ANN

They ain't so bad. Git your nose out of the asphalt someday and maybe you'll learn somethin'.

CORKY

Aw, to hell with it! *(He starts out.)*

LU ANN
Yeah, that's right, go on and go!

CORKY
I'm goin' all right, I'm goin' over to my place, take a shower, change clothes, crank up my old Chivy and come over to your place and take you out to supper.

LU ANN
You are?

CORKY
Damn right! Where do you live?

LU ANN
301 North Grand.

CORKY
Seven okay?

LU ANN
Fine with me.

CORKY
Good. Ah'll see you at seven. We'll go over to Big Spring.

LU ANN
Suits me.

CORKY
See you then. *(He starts to exit, then stops and turns.)* Oh, uh, wear somethin' pink, will you?

LU ANN
Pink! What the hell for?

CORKY
Ah like pink, it's a nice color.

LU ANN
Well la-de-da. Lemme tell you somethin', pal, old Peggy Sue
mighta been a vision of loveliness in pink, but old Lu Ann in
pink looks like somethin' you win at a carnival.

CORKY
Oh, well, hell with it, wear what you want then.

LU ANN
Thanks bunches.

CORKY
Seven, right.

LU ANN
Right. *(He exits. She stands watching the door for a moment,
then calls out)* Hey, Red!

RED
(Entering.) Whattayou want?

LU ANN
What kinda name is Oberlander?

RED
Hell, I don't know. German?

LU ANN
Yeah, maybe so. Hum, Oberlander—Corky Oberlander, by
gollies, that's a right pretty name, don't you think?

RED
Who gives a damn.

ACT III

The time is 1973 in the Hampton home. Few changes in the furnishings. New slipcovers, maybe, and a television set in place of the radio. The rabbit ears on top of the set are covered with aluminum foil.

As the scene begins, CHARMAINE *is lying on the sofa reading a magazine. She is the ACT I image of* LU ANN. *Small, blond, and pretty. She wears a mini-skirt and a sweater. Her transistor radio blares out rock music. The upstage door opens and* SKIP *appears. Time, wear, and booze have taken their toll of* SKIP. *His hair has grayed, he wears thick glasses, and his hands shake. Across his neck is the scar from his suicide attempt, which he makes no effort to conceal. He wears a faded flannel shirt and oversized pants. He crosses to the table and sits down.*

SKIP

For Christ's sake, Charmaine, turn that damn thing off. My head's flat splittin' in two.

CHARMAINE

Aw, go to hell!

SKIP

Aw, please. My head hurts. Ah'm sick.

CHARMAINE

That's tough!

SKIP

I'm gonna tell your ma. Jest see if ah don't.

CHARMAINE

Who gives a damn.

SKIP

Aw, please. That noise is killin' me.

CHARMAINE

Oh, all right. *(Clicks off radio.)*

SKIP

How you kids can stand that noise is beyond me.

CHARMAINE

Maybe it's because we don't stay up all night messin' up our heads with fortified Thunderbird.

SKIP

I wasn't drinkin'! Ah ain't touched no wine in a long, long time.

CHARMAINE

Shore, shore.

SKIP

It's the God's truth.

CHARMAINE

Then how come you were in the bathroom all mornin' with your head in the commode. Hell, they could hear you gaggin' plumb over to Big Spring.

SKIP

A lot you know, a lot you know. When you drink for a long time and then stop, your stomach shrinks up and you get the mornin' sickness.

CHARMAINE

The mornin' sickness! You're crazy; the only people that gits the mornin' sickness is pregnant women.

SKIP

You're the one that's crazy. Pregnant women git the varicose veins, that's all.

CHARMAINE

The varicose veins?

SKIP

It's caused by lack of iron in the blood cells.

CHARMAINE

Boy, are you dumb—whoever told you that?

SKIP

Ah saw it on the television.

CHARMAINE

That's the dumbest thing ah ever heard.

SKIP

Ah saw it, ah tell you.

CHARMAINE

Oh, you never saw nuthin'. You were probably jest havin' them delirium tremors again.

SKIP

Ah ain't never had them things!

CHARMAINE

Oh no? What about the time you said the bullfrogs was after you.

SKIP

Ah don't remember nuthin' about it.

CHARMAINE

That had to be one of the funniest things ah ever seen in mah life. "Help, help, the whole house is full of bullfrogs."

SKIP

You're makin' this all up.

CHARMAINE

"Git 'em off me, git 'em off me! The whole house is full of bullfrogs!"

SKIP

Keep it up, Miss Smarty Pants, just go on and keep it up and ah'm gonna tell on you.

CHARMAINE

Who gives a hoot what you tell.

SKIP

I know somethin'. Boy, do I know somethin' on you.

CHARMAINE

You don't know nuthin' at all.

SKIP

Oh yes, ah do.

CHARMAINE

Oh—yeah, like what?

SKIP

Like what you and Charles Black was doin' out to Lake Brad-leyville last Saturday afternoon.

CHARMAINE

You weren't out there.

SKIP
Ah was so, too.

CHARMAINE
Weren't.

SKIP
Was too. Ah was helpin' old Bowdwin Cassidy out to his bait stand and ah seen you.

CHARMAINE
Boy, what a big fat lie.

SKIP
It ain't either.

CHARMAINE
It just so happens that Charles and me was parked plumb across the lake from Bowdwin's bait stand, so you couldn't have seen a danged thing.

SKIP
Oh no? *(He mimes putting a pair of binoculars to his eyes.)* Peek-a-boo.

CHARMAINE
Do you mean to tell me that you and that damned smelly old Bowdwin Cassidy stood around and spied on Charles and me through binoculars!

SKIP
Gotcha there, don't I; boy, I really gotcha there.

CHARMAINE
Ah oughta slap your ears off you! You dirty old sneak.

SKIP
You better not try nuthin' like that or ah'll tell. Ah'll tell what me and Bowdwin seen.

CHARMAINE
Well, go ahead. Nobody's gonna believe an old busybody like Bowdwin, and ever'body knows you're crazy.

SKIP
Ah'm not neither.

CHARMAINE
Stupid as a cattle guard. Crazy Skip Hampton.

SKIP
You shouldn't oughta call me names that way.

CHARMAINE
Ever'body in town calls you them names—jest because you're my uncle, ah don't see why ah cain't. *(Shouts out window)* Crazy Skip Hampton!

SKIP
Them people in town calls me them names 'cause they're skeered of me.

CHARMAINE
Skeered of you! Boy, that's a hot one. Man, there ain't nuthin' skeered of you.

SKIP
They are skeered of me 'cause ah have killed people.

CHARMAINE
Baloney!

SKIP
In the war, ah killed 'em in the war, lots of people!

CHARMAINE
Run for your lives, ever'body, here comes crazy old Skip.

SKIP

Don't say that! Lu Ann told you not to call me that no more.

CHARMAINE

And the Crazy Man Award of 1973 goes to Skip Hampton!

SKIP

I'm gonna tell your mama on you!

CHARMAINE

Why don't you tell my daddy, you and him was big pals in the Civil War or somethin', why don't you tell him?

SKIP

Ah don't know where he is any more. He used to come and visit me sometimes, but ah don't know where he is any more.

CHARMAINE

Well, ah know where he is. Ah went and seen him one time.

SKIP

Aw, you never either.

CHARMAINE

Ah did so, too! Ah heerd that he was workin' for Hubbard Brothers over to San Angelo, so ah got Charles Black to drive me over there and ah seen him.

SKIP

You shouldn't have done that.

CHARMAINE

Why not? Ah got a right to see mah own real daddy, ain't ah? Anyways, ah never talked to him or nuthin'. Ah jest had a feller point him out to me and ah seen him, that's all.

SKIP

How did he look?

CHARMAINE
Fat.

SKIP
Fat?

CHARMAINE
That's right. Old, fat, and kind of dumb-lookin', you know.
God, what a letdown. Ah don't know what ah was lookin' for,
but it damn sure weren't no dumb fat slob, leanin' up agin
a smelly old semi smokin' a cigarette and probably thinkin'
about nuthin' at all.

SKIP
Now, listen here, Charmaine. Dale was one damned good old
boy and don't you forgit it.

CHARMAINE
Don't forgit it? Aw, cool it, Uncle Bullfrog, ah already have.
(She goes back to her magazine.)

*(LU ANN appears on the front porch carrying two large bags
of groceries. Now in her late thirties, LU ANN is stouter and
mellowed. Her beauty is placid and matronly. She wears a
white uniform with her name over the pocket; on the back of
the uniform is a blue wagon wheel with Howdy Wagon
printed around it.)*

LU ANN
Somebody open the door.

CHARMAINE
(To SKIP) You do it.

SKIP
Do it yourself, smarty pants.

CHARMAINE
Go to hell!

SKIP
Same to you!

LU ANN
Somebody open this damn door!

SKIP
Okay, okay, ah'm comin'. *(He opens the screen door.)*

LU ANN
Thanks. *(Crossing to kitchen.)* Ah heard loud voices comin'
outta here. You two ain't been fightin' again, have you? *(She
enters kitchen.)*

SKIP
Ah'm gonna tell on you.

CHARMAINE
Who cares.

SKIP
You got that dress on she don't like.

CHARMAINE
So what!

LU ANN
(Entering room.) Whooee, ah'm bushed! Charmaine, get off
your lazy can and put them groceries away.

CHARMAINE
Aw hell.

LU ANN
Git!

CHARMAINE
Oh, all right. *(Getting up.)*

LU ANN
What are you doin' with that damned mini-skirt on?

CHARMAINE
Ah'm only wearin' it around the house.

LU ANN
Well, you better. If ah catch you outside in that thing, ah'm
gonna paddle somebody's mini butt!

CHARMAINE
Oh, God, Mama, you are absolutely crude. *(She goes into the
kitchen.)*

LU ANN
Right on, sister! *(She sits on the sofa and removes her shoes.)*
Oh, mah aching feet. Hell, ah bet we said howdy to fifteen
new families today.

SKIP
Big Spring is shore gittin' big.

LU ANN
Shore is. You look in on Mama today?

SKIP
Yeah. She's okay.

LU ANN
Give her any dinner?

SKIP
Shore, shore.

LU ANN
Empty her bedpan?

SKIP
Ah don't like to do that.

LU ANN
Ah know, ah know. But it's got to be done.

SKIP
Ah don't like it, Lu Ann, ah really don't. It makes me throw up.

LU ANN
Well, ah'll do it later.

SKIP
Mah stomach jest turns over and over and . . .

LU ANN
Ah'll take care of it after supper. What did you do today?

SKIP
Oh, nuthin'. Watched the television for a while.

LU ANN
Anythin' good on?

SKIP
Henry Fonda was on the afternoon Old West Movie.

LU ANN
That's nice. You, uh, you didn't feel sick again, did you?

SKIP
No.

LU ANN
Well, if you feel up to it tomorrow, that front grass shore needs a good mowin'.

SKIP

Ah'll git on it first thing. Ah was thinkin' too that ah could clear out a little patch over by the shed and put us in some tomaters and okrie.

LU ANN

Fine.

SKIP

We could have 'em fresh off the vine, wouldn't that be nice?

LU ANN

Shore would.

SKIP

Shore. Ah'm gonna git right on that. First thing in the mornin'. Uh, Lu Ann, seein' as how ah'm gonna do all that tomorrow, do you think that maybe tonight you could, uh, maybe?

LU ANN

No! No money, Skip.

SKIP

Well, no, no. Ah was jest thinkin', if ah had maybe a dollar or somethin', ah could have me mah supper over to the Dixie Dinette, then you won't have to go through no trouble a-fixin' me nuthin'.

LU ANN

Now, you know ah keep a tab down there so's you can git you a cheeseburger or a chicken-fried any time you want. All you gotta do is sign for it.

SKIP

Well, ah know, but maybe if ah go over to Rufe Phelps's place to play a little dominoes, then ah could use a little money, don't you reckin?

LU ANN

Now, Skip honey, you know ah cain't give you no spendin' money.

SKIP

(Whining with childish logic) Why not? Why cain't ah? Ah ain't gonna do nuthin' bad. Why cain't ah even have a dollar in mah pocket? A by-God dollar to buy somethin' with, somethin' ah see in the store—a Coke or a Mars bar or somethin'. Play a little dominoes or maybe go to the picture show. Jest some pocket change to rattle, buy some cigarettes outta the machine, git me an ice-cream soda or a magazine there at Billberry's Drugstore. Jest stuff like that, Lu Ann, that's all. Ah won't buy me no wine, no, sir, not even a beer. They won't let me in Red's place no more. They won't even let me in the door. How can ah git a drink when ah cain't even git in the door? No, ma'am, there jest ain't no way.

LU ANN

You said all this before, Skip. Said you didn't want a drink and couldn't git one. But you did git it, honey, cain't you remember? You got enough to put you in the state hospital in Terrell. You wanna go back up to Terrell?

SKIP

No! No, ah don't wanna go there no more. It was ugly there and them doctors was mean. They put me in a little room and it was cold. They put me in a cage like them chinchillas ah had once. You recollect them chinchillas, Lu Ann, and when it was cold?

LU ANN

Sure, honey. Ah remember, but that's all over now, all gone. We ain't gonna talk about them mean times any more, are we?

SKIP

No, no more mean times.

LU ANN
Wanna watch the television for a while? The Country Jubilee
Show'll be on tonight.

SKIP
No. Ah think maybe ah'll go on over to the dinette for mah
supper, but ah'm not gonna have no cheeseburger or chick-
en-fry, ah'm gonna have me an enchilada, then ah'll sign the
tab. Sign the tab jest like you said. You know, Lu Ann, it's a
funny thing how things boil down, ain't it?

LU ANN
Whattayou mean, Skip?

SKIP
When all that stands between a man and the by-God loony
bin is his sister's tab down to the Dixie Dinette.

CHARMAINE
(Entering from the kitchen.) My Gawd, you know, we got
them big red piss ants under the sink again?

LU ANN
Ah'll pick up some bug killer tomorrow.

CHARMAINE
Terrific. Maybe Uncle Skip will chug it down with his mornin' bowl of Cream of Wheat.

LU ANN
Charmaine, that's enough of that. Now, if you got schoolwork
to do, why don't you go on up to your room and do it.

CHARMAINE
Can ah take mah radio with me?

LU ANN
Ah don't care. Jest don't play it too loud—you might disturb
your grandma.

SKIP

She won't do her homework if she's got that radio.

CHARMAINE

You go to hell!

SKIP

You hear that? Cussin', cussin' at me!

LU ANN

Now that's a by-God 'nuff!

SKIP

She's got that skirt on that you don't like.

CHARMAINE

He's always pickin' on me!

LU ANN

Git on upstairs!

CHARMAINE

Ever'body picks on me! What the hell kinda chance do ah have around here anyway, what with a crazy uncle, a dumb-lookin' daddy, and the goddamned Howdy Wagon for a mama! *(She turns and exits, slamming the door.)*

SKIP

She went over to San Angelo and saw old Dale.

LU ANN

Yeah, I know. Charlie Black's mama told me about it.

SKIP

She said he was fat and dumb-lookin'.

LU ANN

Yeah, well. What'd she expect me to find here in Bradleyville in 1953, the by-God King of England. *(Pause.)* Ah thought you was goin' on down to the dinette.

SKIP
Ah'm goin', ah'm goin'. You know, Lu Ann, ah was thinkin' it might be nice if ah could maybe leave a little tip.

LU ANN
Oh, for Christ's sake!

SKIP
It would be nice now, and you know it. Leave maybe fifty cents there on the counter.

LU ANN
Git on outta here—ah'm tired of lookin' at you.

SKIP
Ah'm goin'.

*(A figure approaches the porch—*SKIP *sees him and stops.)*

LU ANN
Well, what's keepin' you?

SKIP
Somebody's comin'.

LU ANN
Probably one of Charmaine's skinny boyfriends.

SKIP
Nope, it's a grown man.

(There is a knock at the door.)

LU ANN
I'll git it. *(She walks to the door.)* What can ah do for you?

BILLY BOB
Mrs. Oberlander?

LU ANN
Yes.

BILLY BOB
Mrs. Lu Ann Hampton Oberlander?

LU ANN
Mrs. Lu Ann Hampton *Laverty* Oberlander, if you want the whole damn handle. Who are you?

BILLY BOB
Ah'm Billy Bob, Billy Bob Wortman.

LU ANN
Billy Bob! Well, Jesus Christ on a crutch. Come on in this house and let me look at you. *(She opens the door and lets* BILLY BOB *in. He wears a black suit and horn-rimmed glasses. His hair is stylishly mod and he now sports a small mustache.)* Lookee here, Skip, it's old Billy Bob—the old preacher boy himself.

SKIP
(Shaking hands.) Howdy, Billy Bob.

BILLY BOB
Hello, Skip, how are you?

SKIP
Fine, fine.

LU ANN
Well, sit down, Billy Bob, or do we call you Reverend nowadays?

BILLY BOB

No, no, just Billy Bob. Plain old Billy Bob. *(He notices* LU ANN*'s bare feet—she sees this and scurries back to her chair to put her shoes on.)*

LU ANN

Well, sit down, plain old Billy Bob. Make yourself at home. God, it's good to see you.

BILLY BOB

Well, it's marvelous to see you, Lu Ann.

LU ANN

Marvelous? Listen to that, Skip, listen to mah little old high-school boyfriend usin' them big words.

SKIP

Sounds pretty good.

LU ANN

You wanna cup of coffee or somethin'?

BILLY BOB

No, nothing thanks.

LU ANN

Sit down, Skip. Quit hangin' around back there.

SKIP

Ah better be gittin' on down to the dinette, Lu Ann. *(To* BILLY BOB*)* Ah'm havin' me an enchilada tonight.

LU ANN

(Rising and crossing to him.) Now, Skip, you're comin' right on home now, hear me?

SKIP

Yeah, ah'll be right on back in.

LU ANN
Well, don't . . . you know.

SKIP
Ah know, ah know. See you all later. *(He exits.)*

LU ANN
(Looking out of door.) God, ah hope he don't . . .

BILLY BOB
I know about Brother Hampton's illness, Lu Ann.

LU ANN
Yeah, well, it's nuthin' to trouble yourself about there, Billy Bob.

BILLY BOB
It's my job to trouble myself, Lu Ann.

LU ANN
What? Oh, hell, ah plumb forgot about you bein' a preacher, Billy Bob. My goodness, imagine that. Well, let me look at you. By gollies, that little old mustache is a dandy, ain't it?

BILLY BOB
Yes, well, my congregation rather likes it: it gives me some dignity, don't you think?

LU ANN
Oh, shore. It shore does.

BILLY BOB
I didn't think you'd recognize me with it on.

LU ANN
Oh pshaw, Billy Bob, ah'd know your old hide if ah saw it hangin' on a fence post. Sit down.

BILLY BOB
Yes, thank you.

LU ANN
You know, Billy Bob, ah was real proud to hear you had graduated over there at the Texas Christian University. Ah was livin' in Snyder at the time and my mama wrote me all about it, even sent me the clippings from the *Bradleyville Record.*

BILLY BOB
Well, that's nice.

LU ANN
Oh, shore. Ah even read about you gittin' married. You married a Fort Worth girl, didn't you?

BILLY BOB
Yes, I met Maxine in school. She's a fine woman.

LU ANN
Well, ah jest bet she is. Now, let's see, you have three or is it four children, Billy Bob?

BILLY BOB
Four. Four fine boys.

LU ANN
Well, ain't that nice.

BILLY BOB
You just have the one girl, don't you?

LU ANN
Yes, little Charmaine. Well now, listen to me say *little* Charmaine. She's nearly a growed-up woman now.

BILLY BOB
How old is she?

LU ANN
Seventeen. Can you imagine?

BILLY BOB
My, my.

LU ANN
Yes, she's a chore sometimes, but mostly she's a blessin'. Ah've really got a kick outta watchin' her grow up. Spoiled the devil out of her. But, shoot, what are kids for if it ain't to spoil a little bit?

BILLY BOB
Yes, my boys can be quite the little rascals sometimes too.

LU ANN
Ah wish sometimes that Corky and me coulda give her a little brother or sister—but, well, it jest weren't meant to be.

BILLY BOB
Yes, my mother wrote me about the accident—a real tragedy.

LU ANN
Yes, it was, we wasn't married but a couple of years when it happened. He was out on the job, you see, when his pickup was hit by one of them road machines.

BILLY BOB
Was he killed instantly?

LU ANN
No, he lived for about six or eight hours. 'Course he was busted up so bad there weren't much hope. They got him over to the county hospital and he passed away there. Ah got to see him once affore he died.

BILLY BOB
That was a blessing.

LU ANN
Yes, it was. They had him in a room with these curtains all around. Poor old Corky, he was all bandaged up with tubes and bottles all over him. When ah got there he opened his eyes and moved his hand a little bit and sorter motioned to me, so ah bent down close to his head and he whispered to me real low like, "Lu Ann, Lu Ann, it hit me again, a buffalo, the biggest goddamn buffalo ah ever seed."

BILLY BOB
What did he mean?

LU ANN
Oh, it was just sort of an old joke we had.

BILLY BOB
You ever think of marrying again?

LU ANN
Oh, Lordy, no. Right after Corky was killed Mama had her stroke and ah jest sorter settled in to look after her. Ah had already quit my job at the beauty shop so ah got me this-here job drivin' the Howdy Wagon over to Big Spring.

BILLY BOB
You like the work?

LU ANN
Shore. 'Course ah gotta drive over there of a mornin', but it's not far. And then I like meetin' new people. We git names of new folks movin' into town, you see, and then we drive the Howdy Wagon over to their house and hand out these-here free coupons.

BILLY BOB
What are they good for?

LU ANN
Why, all sorts of thangs. Free bucket of Colonel Sanders'
Kentucky Fried Chicken, two free bundles of wash at the
Washateria, free round of miniature golf, five gallons of Fina
gasoline, six-pack of Coors beer . . . oops, shouldn't of said
that, ah reckin.

BILLY BOB
That's okay.

LU ANN
Well, anyway, all sorts of thangs like that. It's to help the new
folks git on to the town, you see.

BILLY BOB
Yes, I understand.

LU ANN
Where do you live now, Billy Bob?

BILLY BOB
Kansas City.

LU ANN
Well, think of that. How do you like the big-city life?

BILLY BOB
We like it very much. I have a fine church there, fine congregation.

LU ANN
Well, ah jest bet you do.

BILLY BOB
Yes, it's nice to be settled down for a while. I'm afraid I've

put my family through quite some strain moving around all these years. You knew that I was in missionary work, didn't you?

LU ANN
Ah heard somethin' about it.

BILLY BOB
Oh, yes, indeed. We're here for a little visit. So when I heard you were in town, why, I just had to look you and your mother up. You're about the last of the old high-school gang that's still left around.

LU ANN
Yeah, nobody stays in the little towns any more.

CHARMAINE
(Offstage) Mama, I cain't work these goddamn algebra problems!

LU ANN
Well, figger it out for yourself. I got company down here.

CHARMAINE
Who?

LU ANN
Billy Bob Wortman.

CHARMAINE
Who the hell's that?

LU ANN
An old friend of mine from high school.

CHARMAINE
Big deal!

(Sound of a door slamming.)

LU ANN
Confounded kids. Come out on the porch, Billy Bob, ah believe it's a little cooler.

BILLY BOB
Fine.

(They stand for a moment looking out.)

BILLY BOB
Bradleyville. Do they still put the Christmas lights on the water tower every year?

LU ANN
Shore.

BILLY BOB
I guess nothing much has changed in town, has it?

LU ANN
Oh, we have a few new things.

BILLY BOB
Sure enough?

LU ANN
Uh-huh. The Dairy Queen put in a new parking lot and the drive-in's got *two* screens now.

BILLY BOB
Boy, old Pete Honeycutt would have loved that.

LU ANN
Yeah, ah reckon. Let's see now, the bank's got a whole new front on it, and then of course there's always Mumford County Estates.

BILLY BOB
What's that?

LU ANN
Oh, that's a lake-development outfit we got out to Lake Brad-leyville.

BILLY BOB
Really?

LU ANN
Shore. Floyd Kinkaid and Clarence Sickenger got 'em a whole bunch of homes and boathouses and such like out there.

BILLY BOB
Well, that's progress, I guess.

LU ANN
Shore is. They were gonna put 'em in a golf course but they couldn't get the grass to grow!

BILLY BOB
You know, it's funny, Lu Ann, but I never figured you would stay here in Bradleyville.

LU ANN
Ah did leave once. Got as far as Snyder. Aw, I don't know, Billy Bob, ah spoze ah never did think much further than this-here town—never hankered to. You recollect that time when you and me was spozed to go on the senior picnic and ah run out on you and went to San Angelo with old Dale Laverty?

BILLY BOB
I'll never forget it—my heart was broken for a whole week.

LU ANN
Well, ah think maybe it was then that mah life jest sorter dug

itself in. Kindly found its little hollow to stay in. You went on to the college and all them other places, but I jest started a-standin' still. Ah run out on a picnic and ran straight into a rut, you might say—even old Corky couldn't pull me outta it, bless his soul.

BILLY BOB

Oh, I don't know, Lu Ann, there isn't really a lot more in the big cities that isn't right here in Bradleyville.

LU ANN

How's come you never played any basketball while you was there at T.C.U.?

BILLY BOB

My word, you had to be good to play ball there. I was just a little old Bradleyville boy, just wasn't up to snuff.

LU ANN

But you was good, Billy Bob, you was real good.

BILLY BOB

Oh, not really.

LU ANN

But ah recollect you playin' over to Snyder that time—mah, how I used to cheer for you. You recall that, Billy Bob, and the time you-all dyed your hair green?

BILLY BOB

Well, that was a long time ago.

LU ANN

You know, mah mama once told me that them times would be the happiest of mah life, and lookin' back on it all, ah believe she mighta been right. Lordy, but it was fun, wasn't it, Billy Bob? The pep rallies, the bonfires, all them dances . . .

BILLY BOB
Paintin' up them posters when Pete Honeycutt ran for president of the senior class.

LU ANN
Mary Beth Johnson, Eveline Blair, and me leadin' the cheers. Goin' over to the Billberry's Drugstore after the home games with Pete and Ruthie Lee Lawell . . .

BILLY BOB
For chocolate Cokes.

LU ANN
That's right! Pickin' on poor old Milo Crawford. Remember all that, Billy Bob? You know, sometimes when ah'm here alone, ah get out my old Bradleyville High yearbook and just go through it lookin' at them pictures and rememberin'. You ever do that?

BILLY BOB
It's a waste of the Lord's time to dwell on the past, Lu Ann.

LU ANN
Oh, pshaw. The Lord's got lots of time to waste. It's us the clock runs down on! You know, Billy Bob, it's a funny thing, but ah'm about the same age mah mama was when you and me was in high school. My God, ain't that somethin'? It's like ah was her and Charmaine was me and ever'body around us got old and different lookin'.

BILLY BOB
Am I so old and different lookin'?

LU ANN
Oh, no, no, of course not. That's one thing about dwellin' in the past. People you loved back then stay the same. You're still old sweet-smilin', goof-off, green-headed Billy Bob Wortman. That preacher suit and mustache don't fool me none.

BILLY BOB
Yes, well. I haven't really got a lot of time left, Lu Ann. Do you think I could see your mother now?

LU ANN
Why shore. My gosh, here ah am runnin' off at the mouth as usual. Ah'll bring her right on out. We keep her in the down-stairs bedroom now because of the wheelchair. *(She goes to the up-center door.)* She don't recognize people much any more, so don't feel bad now if she don't know you.

BILLY BOB
Yes, of course, I understand.

(LU ANN exits. BILLY BOB looks at his watch and fidgets about the room. He glances through CHARMAINE's magazine and drops it distastefully. LU ANN re-enters with CLAUDINE in the wheelchair. Her hair is totally white, her waxen hands lie limply on her lap. The stroke has paralyzed one side of her face and uncontrollable saliva drools from her mouth, which LU ANN wipes away from time to time with a clean handkerchief.)

LU ANN
Here we are. You got a visitor, Mama. Billy Bob Wortman's come all the way from Kansas City for a little visit, ain't that nice? You remember Billy Bob Wortman, don't you, Mama?

BILLY BOB
How are you, Mrs. Hampton?

LU ANN
Why, she's jest as fine as she can be, aren't you, Mama? Be up and outta this old wheelchair just any old day now. Don't you know Billy Bob, Mama? Mah old boyfriend from high school, he's come a long way to see you and say howdy.

(CLAUDINE gives no sign of recognition at all; simply stares straight ahead.)

BILLY BOB
(Taking CLAUDINE*'s hand.)* Hello there, Mrs. Hampton, how are you? *(Nothing— He drops her hand.)* Can she speak at all, Lu Ann?

LU ANN
No, not a word since her stroke. Ah think that's the biggest shame of the whole business, her not bein' able to talk, 'cause that's one thing Mama loved to do. Couldn't sew, hated to cook, and never read nuthin' but the funny papers, but, oh my, how she loved to talk.

BILLY BOB
Will she be like this from now on—I mean, what do the doctors say?

LU ANN
They say she ain't never goin' to come outta this, not on this earth anyway. So ah jest keep her clean an' fed and ah look after her the best way ah kin.

BILLY BOB
You know, Lu Ann, there are homes for people in her condition. I could look into the church home in Sweetwater if you like.

LU ANN
This is her home, Billy Bob.

BILLY BOB
Well, yes, I know, but it must be a terrible burden.

LU ANN
Aw, it ain't so bad, at least thisaway the burden is mostly on my body—if ah sent her off somewhere, the burden would be on my heart. You know, Billy Bob, them doctors told me that Mama would be a vegetable for the rest of her life—can you imagine that? A vegetable! Hell, my mama ain't no vegetable, she's a flower, a great old big pretty flower.

BILLY BOB
Yes, a creature of God.

LU ANN
You bet.

BILLY BOB
Well, Lu Ann, I really must be going now.

LU ANN
Yep, ah speck them boys will be a-missin' their daddy.

BILLY BOB
It was fine to see you again, Lu Ann.

LU ANN
Well, it was all mah pleasure, Billy Bob. Don't be such a
stranger any more, you come on back any time and bring the
missus and them boys, you hear?

BILLY BOB
Yes, I'll do that. Well, goodbye, Lu Ann, and may the Lord
stay by your side.

LU ANN
So long, Billy Bob, and may, uh . . . may you have lots of luck.
(BILLY BOB *exits.* LU ANN *stands for a moment watching out
the screen door, then she turns and comes back into the
room.)* Well now, weren't that somethin', Mama? Who would
have guessed that one day old Billy Bob would have him a
church way up in Kansas City. Jest cain't ever tell, can you,
Mama? Jest cain't ever tell. Oh, hell, look at the time, we
done missed most of the Country Jubilee. *(She crosses to the
television.)* You know, Mama, if ah'd have played mah cards
right ah probably could have been Mrs. Billy Bob Wortman
today. That's right, missionary's wife way up there in Kansas
City, helpin' to spread the Word. *(She giggles.)* But, you

know, Mama, ah jest never could cotton to that boy's name. Billy Bob Wortman. Why, it's jest plain silly-soundin'. *(She flicks on the set.)*

(The lights dim as the twang of country music floods into the room.)

The Oldest
Living Graduate

Characters

COLONEL J. C. KINKAID *Seventy-five. Eccentric World War I vet and oldest living graduate of Mirabeau B. Lamar Military Academy*

FLOYD KINKAID *Forty-two. The Colonel's son*

MAUREEN KINKAID *Forty-two. The Colonel's daughter-in-law*

CLARENCE SICKENGER *Forty-three. A friend of Floyd's*

MARTHA ANN SICKENGER *Twenty-seven. Clarence's wife*

MIKE TREMAINE *Forty-nine. A hired hand*

MAJOR LEROY W. KETCHUM *Fifty. Commandant of the military school*

CADET WHOPPER TURNBULL *Seventeen. A student at the academy*

CLAUDINE HAMPTON *Forty-nine. A practical nurse*

ACT I
Scene 1

The time is the summer of 1962 in Bradleyville. The setting is the den of FLOYD KINKAID *'s plush ranch-style home on the outskirts of town. The den itself has a rich masculine decor. A door, stage left, leads to the living room. Upstage is the door leading to the patio. An archway, stage right, leads to the* COLONEL *'s bedroom. Next to the patio door are a large leather armchair and a footstool. In one corner are a small desk and a chair. Above the desk are many framed photographs—one of the* COLONEL *in his World War I uniform, another of* FRANKLIN KINKAID *in a World War II flying suit, and many smaller photos, mainly of ranch scenes. Above the smaller photos is a long picture of a group of men on the steps of a building. On the picture is the caption:* Knights of the White Magnolia Convention, Tulsa, Oklahoma, 1939. *In another corner of the room is a gun rack with a stuffed deer head over it. The gun case can be opened to reveal a well-stocked bar. Next to the rack are two wood-and-leather chairs. There are Indian rugs on the floor and draped over the chairs.*

As the curtain goes up we hear the COLONEL *'s voice calling from his bedroom.*

COLONEL
(Offstage) Floyd! . . . Floyd! . . . Floyd! *(Entering in his wheelchair.)* Goddamn it, Floyd, where the hell are you?

MAUREEN

(Offstage) I'll be right back, Martha Ann. *(Entering from the living room.)* What's the matter, Colonel?

COLONEL

Where the hell is Floyd? He promised to take me for a drive today.

MAUREEN

Floyd's gone into town for a while.

COLONEL

What the hell for?

MAUREEN

He and Clarence Sickenger had to go to the bank.

COLONEL

Clarence Sickenger? If there was ever a boy born dumb, he is it. What the hell is Floyd hangin' around with him for?

MAUREEN

They're goin' into some sort of business deal together.

COLONEL

Hell! Now ah'll never git to go for a drive. Who's that you were gabbin' with out there in the livin' room? Sounded like a by-God hen house out there.

MAUREEN

Martha Ann. She's stayin' here till Floyd and Clarence git back.

COLONEL

Who?

MAUREEN

Martha Ann Sickenger, damnit. Clarence's wife.

COLONEL
Never heard of her.

MAUREEN
Why, of course you have. Her folks own the feed store downtown.

COLONEL
She musta been a Montgomery then.

MAUREEN
That's right.

COLONEL
Probably old John Montgomery's daughter.

MAUREEN
Granddaughter.

COLONEL
Yeah. Well, what the hell. Ah knew old John Montgomery. Nice quiet sort of feller.

MAUREEN
Well, his granddaughter damned sure isn't. She's been borin' me to death all afternoon. I've never heard so much gossip in mah life.

MARTHA ANN
(Offstage) Maureen!

MAUREEN
Oh, God! Why don't you just go on back and watch your television set, Colonel. I'll call you when Floyd gits back.

COLONEL
Well, by God he better not take all day about it. Ah wanna go for a drive and that's all there is to it! *(He exits.)*

MARTHA ANN
(Sticking her head in the door.) What's goin on in here?

MAUREEN
Nothing, Martha Ann.

MARTHA ANN
Didn't ah hear the Colonel talkin' about somethin'?

MAUREEN
It's possible.

MARTHA ANN
How's he doin' these days?

MAUREEN
You got ears, haven't you. He gripes and grumbles around here all day long.

MARTHA ANN
Ah thought you and Floyd was gonna get a day nurse to look after him.

MAUREEN
Oh, we tried. The Colonel runs through them nurses like peanuts. Sent all the way to Forth Worth for the last one and he had her run outta here in less than an hour.

MARTHA ANN
Y'know, Maureen, Clarence says the only place that can handle shell-shock business like the Colonel has is a veterans hospital.

MAUREEN
Oh, he doesn't cause me that much trouble. Ida Ruth does all the cooking and housework and Mike Tremaine is always handy if anything really serious comes up.

MARTHA ANN

Well, ah wouldn't put up with it. Saddled down with a crabby old man like that.

MAUREEN

Yeah, well, he gits on my nerves sometimes but it does break up the monotony. That is, if anything could break up the monotony of this damned little town.

MARTHA ANN

Oh, my word, Maureen, the things you say. Why, ah just love livin' here in Bradleyville, and jest all sorts of fun things happen here. Why, just the other day ah was at my study club meeting and in walks old Mavis Purnell in a full-length mink coat from Neiman and Marcus. Well, ah . . .

MAUREEN

Oh, for God's sake, Martha Ann. Please do me a favor and don't get started on all that damned gossip again.

MARTHA ANN

Well, after all, Maureen, you said you wanted to know.

MAUREEN

I did what?

MARTHA ANN

You said you wanted to know what goes on here in Bradleyville.

MAUREEN

My God.

MARTHA ANN

Anyway, here's Mavis Purnell with that old horsy face and bony legs stickin' out of thousands of dollars of fur coat. Ah mean, it done nothin' for her. Absolutely nothin' at all.

MAUREEN
(Yawning.) How did she get old Dean Purnell to come up
with the cash for a new coat?

MARTHA ANN
She caught him runnin' around with a little old bouncy-
butted barmaid from Big Spring.

MAUREEN
My God, you wouldn't think Dean could get it up with a
block and tackle, much less have enough to play games with
a barmaid.

MARTHA ANN
(Laughing.) A block and tackle! Ah'm going to have to tell
that one to the girls at the study club!

MAUREEN
Oh, please do.

(The COLONEL *appears at door in his wheelchair.)*

COLONEL
While you're at it, you can tell 'em somethin' for me: "Cack-
lin' roosters and crowin' hens come to no good end."

MAUREEN
Just go on back and watch the television, Colonel. Aren't they
showin' them reruns of the cattle-drive show?

COLONEL
(Entering.) Sick of that damned show. Sick of it! They're
spozed to be drivin' three thousand head or such-like and the
same old crooked-horned spotted steer has gone by the
screen forty-two times. Ah think they only got about twenty-
five cattle out there and the bumble-dickin' trail boss keeps
gripin' about bein' shorthanded.

MARTHA ANN
Hello there, Colonel Kinkaid.

COLONEL
(Peering at her.) Who are you?

MARTHA ANN
Martha Ann Sickenger.

COLONEL
Oh, shore, shore. Martha Ann Montgomery. Pretty little thing, ain't you?

MARTHA ANN
(Flattered) Well, ah hope so, Colonel.

COLONEL
Then how's come you married that dumb-butted Clarence Sickenger!

MARTHA ANN
Well, ah, uh . . .

COLONEL
Sometimes the pretty ones ain't so smart, are they? How's come your folks let you get hung up with Clarence Sickenger?

MARTHA ANN
Well, uh . . .

COLONEL
Thought old John Montgomery would have more sense than to let a daughter of his marry a Sickenger. You didn't let yourself git in the family way before the wedding, did you?

MARTHA ANN
Of course not!

COLONEL
Huh. Must have been the money then. You got any kids there, Martha Ann?

MARTHA ANN
Yes, sir, two.

COLONEL
Well, good for you. At least Old Clarence is good for somethin'. Floyd and Maureen here ain't got nary a nuthin'.

MAUREEN
Damnit now, Colonel, don't get started on that again.

COLONEL
Kept hopin' ah would have me some grandkids someday, but anybody with eyes in his head can see that it's too damn late now.

MAUREEN
Hell with it! Come on, Martha Ann, let's go into the livin' room.

COLONEL
Yes, sir, it's too damn late now.

MAUREEN
Go on, Martha Ann! *(MARTHA ANN exits toward the living room; MAUREEN turns at the door.)* Keep it up, Colonel, ever' time you open your mouth you're talkin' yourself one step closer to the old soldiers' home. *(She exits.)*

COLONEL
(Muttering) Floyd never shoulda married that woman. Barren as a by-God thirty-year-old ewe. *(The phone rings.)* Bumble-dickin' phone! Ah'm comin'. *(The COLONEL wheels his chair over to the phone and picks it up.)* Kinkaid here, who the hell are you? . . . Who? . . . Never heard of you . . . Hell,

yes, this is the Kinkaid residence, where else would ah be!

COLONEL

MAUREEN

(Calling from the living room) Colonel, it's not for you. I got it out here, on the extension.

COLONEL

Damn sure is too for me. Ah answered it, didn't ah! *(Into phone)* If you didn't want to talk to me, then why the hell did you ring up mah house! This better not be one of them-there dirty phone calls . . .

MAUREEN

(From living room) Damnit, Colonel, hang up! The call isn't for you!

COLONEL

You mean it's for you? *(Into phone)* You're a pretty sad-assed sex fiend, feller, if you called over here for Maureen, wasted a by-God dime . . .

MAUREEN

(Appearing at the door.) Will you please get off the line! This happens to be Reverend Stone callin'. He's got a message of some kind for Floyd.

COLONEL

The hell you say. *(Into phone)* Kinkaid here again. By God, Stone, ah'm plumb ashamed of you. What kind of a preacher makes dirty phone calls? You lose the callin' or somethin'? . . .

MAUREEN

(Reaching for the phone.) Gimme that . . .

COLONEL

Git away from here. *(Into phone)* Ah seen a preacher lose the

callin' over there in France. He was holy as hell till we got
into the trenches. Wound up cussin' them whiz-bangs worse
than any of us. Knew more cuss words than old Harry S.
Truman. Never heard "Damnit to hell" said with such by-
God ringin' fervor in mah life . . .

MAUREEN
Now that's jest enough! *(She grabs the receiver out of his
hand.)* Hello . . . Hello . . . He hung up.

COLONEL
Hell, yes, he hung up. Ah let him know the truth of things.

MAUREEN
Good God.

COLONEL
Don't like preachers anyway. *(*MAUREEN *starts to dial.)*
What the hell you doin'?

MAUREEN
I'm goin' to call Reverend Stone back and apologize.

COLONEL
Oh no, you ain't.

MAUREEN
Jest why the hell not?

COLONEL
Cause ah'm mad at preachers, ah don't like 'em any
more.

MAUREEN
I know I'm goin' to feel like a damn fool for askin' this, but
why?

COLONEL
Why what?

MAUREEN
Why don't you like preachers?

COLONEL
What preachers?

MAUREEN
Any preachers!

COLONEL
Who said that?

MAUREEN
You did, damnit! You said you didn't like preachers.

COLONEL
Oh, ah git it. Yessiree, I git it now. You're tryin' to git me in trouble with the Lord.

MAUREEN
What?

COLONEL
You're not only tryin' to kick me outta mah own house, you're tryin' to git me kicked plumb outta the by-God Kingdom of Heaven!

MAUREEN
What in the hell are you talkin' about?

COLONEL
Plumb outta heaven!!

MARTHA ANN
(Coming back into the room.) Maureen, did those green drapes in there come from . . .

COLONEL
Well, ah got news for you, sister. There ain't no way to

keep me outta heaven 'cause ah done served mah term in hell. *(To* MARTHA ANN*)* Betcha didn't know that, did you?

MARTHA ANN
No, uh, Colonel, ah, uh . . .

COLONEL
Well, ah did. Served mah term in hell right over there in the trenches. Over the goddamned top, over the top and the Germans all the time shootin' them damn machine guns, blappity, blappity, blap!

MAUREEN
All right, now, Colonel, jest calm down.

COLONEL
Blappity blap.

MARTHA ANN
(Taking his arm.) Take it easy, Colonel Kinkaid.

COLONEL
Git your hands offen me. Go on home and look after all them damn kids you got. Gonna have the whole town of Bradley-ville full of Sickengers one of these days. Whole county over-run with goofy-lookin' Sickenger kids!

MAUREEN
I'm gonna call Mike Tremaine, he can take you for a drive. *(She opens the patio door and calls out.)* Yoo-hoo, Mike, can you come in here for a minute.

MIKE
(From the yard) Be right there, Mrs. Kinkaid.

MAUREEN
There now, Colonel, Mike can take you anywhere you want to go.

COLONEL
Good. Ah like Mike. He's a nice fella.

(The door opens and MIKE TREMAINE *enters. He is a tall, weather-beaten man.)*

MIKE
What can ah do for you, Miz Kinkaid?

MAUREEN
I hate to interrupt your chores, Mike, but I wonder if you could take the Colonel for a little drive?

MIKE
Be glad to. Hello, Miz Sickenger. Howdy, Colonel Kinkaid.

COLONEL
Howdy there, Mike. Whatcha been up to?

MIKE
Just fixin' on some fence over to the horse barn.

COLONEL
Well, good for you.

MIKE
Where you wanna drive to, Colonel?

COLONEL
Over to mah place on the lake. Ah wanna look at mah town.

MIKE
Okay, Colonel. *(He wheels the* COLONEL *to the patio door.)* Over to the lake it is.

COLONEL
Ah wanna look at mah town!

(They exit.)

MARTHA ANN

My God, Maureen. He's jest terrible. Did you hear some of the things he said to me!

MAUREEN

You! What about Reverend Stone. Poor old guy may never use the telephone again.

MARTHA ANN

What was he talkin' about when he said he wanted to see his town? There isn't any town out to the lake.

MAUREEN

He thinks there is.

MARTHA ANN

Where, for pity sakes?

MAUREEN

You know that spread of land we got out there that the Colonel calls the Genet Farm?

MARTHA ANN

Sure, Clarence has a place right next to it.

MAUREEN

Well, that's where the town's spozed to be. We got all that lake property out there full of nuthin' but brush and jackrabbits. The Colonel won't even let Floyd run any cattle on it.

MARTHA ANN

Then how's come he's gonna give it to Floyd and Clarence?

MAUREEN

The Genet Farm?

MARTHA ANN

Shore. That's what I was fixin' to tell you earlier. That's the land they're gonna develop, right out there along the lake-front.

MAUREEN
Floyd never mentioned a damn thing to me about their deal havin' anythin' to do with that lake property! Are you sure about this?

MARTHA ANN
Uh-huh. Clarence says they're gonna build houses and boat docks and all sorts of things out there. Clarence wants to call it Mumford County Estates.

MAUREEN
Clarence? My God! House and boat docks on the Colonel's Genet Farm. I can't believe it. That old man treats that property like it was sacred. Goes out there all the time.

MARTHA ANN
To look at his "town"?

MAUREEN
That's right.

MARTHA ANN
Boy, that is really spooky. Lookin' at a town that ain't there.

FLOYD	MARTHA ANN
(Ad-libs offstage) Oh, man, is it ever hot out here. Come on in, Clarence. Maureen, Martha Ann, where the hell are you?	There are the boys now!

MAUREEN
We're out in the den, Floyd.

(FLOYD *and* CLARENCE *enter the room.* FLOYD *is a thin, nervous man;* CLARENCE *is large and heavy-set.*)

FLOYD
Howdy, ever'body; where's Dad?

MAUREEN
Mike Tremaine took him for a drive.

FLOYD
Good. Whattayou-all doin' sittin' around out here? How about that, Clarence. I bring in an interior decorator all the way from Houston to redo that damned livin' room and she won't even sit in it.

MAUREEN
I like this room. It's comfortable.

FLOYD
All that dough laid out for that livin' room and nobody even goes in there. Whattayou think of that? *(He opens the gun rack and mixes drinks for himself and* CLARENCE.*)*

CLARENCE
It's a pretty good-lookin' room.

MARTHA ANN
Shore is. Them green drapes in there are about the nicest ah ever seen.

CLARENCE
Them fireplace rocks here come from San Antonio, don't they?

FLOYD
Shore do.

CLARENCE
Ah been meanin' to git a load of them rocks for a barbecue pit ah'm gonna put out on our patio.

MARTHA ANN
Oh, you and that durn barbecue pit. He's been foolin' around with that thing for two years now.

CLARENCE
Who put in your pit, Floyd?

FLOYD
Mike Tremaine and a couple of colored boys.

CLARENCE
After I git them rocks, how about lendin' old Mike to me for about a week?

FLOYD
Shore.

CLARENCE
Ah figger to put that pit right by the swimmin' pool.

FLOYD
That's where we got ours.

CLARENCE
It's a good place for one.

MARTHA ANN
Ah just love barbecue. You gonna have barbecue served at the Founder's Day dinner again, Floyd?

FLOYD
Yeah. Ah got an outfit from Big Spring to bring it all over.

CLARENCE
That Big Spring outfit the same bunch that did the VFW picnic?

FLOYD
That's right. J. B. Kelly put me on to 'em.

CLARENCE
They put out a pretty good spread.

MARTHA ANN
Ah jest wish they wouldn't put the cole slaw in them little paper cups. It just ruins the taste, makes it all waxy-like. Don't you think so, Maureen?

MAUREEN
Well, ah . . .

CLARENCE
What ah don't like are them flimsy little old plastic forks. Hell, ah bet ah broke four of 'em just tryin' to cut a by-God piece of meat.

MARTHA ANN
Come to think of it, that meat was a little stringy.

CLARENCE
Ever notice how them paper plates get a little soggy-like on the bottom?

MARTHA ANN
They shore do. The one ah had dripped barbecue sauce all over mah new dress.

CLARENCE
Found a rock in the beans too.

MAUREEN
Tell you what, Clarence. Next year why don't you and Martha Ann furnish the waxy, rocky, soggy, goddamned barbecue?

CLARENCE
Well, what the hell, Maureen, ah never meant nuthin'.

MARTHA ANN
The sauce was real tasty.

MAUREEN
Shore.

CLARENCE
The coffee was pretty good too.

MAUREEN
Score one for Maxwell House.

CLARENCE
Yeah, well, uh, sure. *(Pause.)* Well, listen, Floyd, ah 'speck Martha Ann and me better be headin' on home now.

MARTHA ANN
Yeah, ah promised to take the kids out ridin' to the country club, they'll be madder than hell if ah don't.

CLARENCE
Ah'll call you tomorrow about our deal, okay?

FLOYD
Shore, that'll be fine. Ah'll see you-all to the door.

CLARENCE
We know the way. Come on, Martha Ann. *(He exits.)*

MARTHA ANN
That sauce was real good, Maureen.

CLARENCE
(Offstage) MARTHA ANN!

(She exits.)

MAUREEN
(*After a slight pause, mimicking* MARTHA ANN) "That sauce was real good, Maureen." Jeezus, I've had that whiny little twang in my ear all day long.

FLOYD
Oh, hell, she never meant nuthin' by all that.

MAUREEN
The devil she didn't. Why are we such big buddies with the Sickengers nowadays? Neither one of us likes 'em very much.

FLOYD
Ah jest thought since we were goin' into this deal together that the families ought to be closer, that's all.

MAUREEN
Sure, closer to the Sickengers and further away from the Colonel. What's all this crap I hear about him givin' his Genet farm to you and Clarence?

FLOYD
Who *told* you about that?

MAUREEN
Martha Ann.

FLOYD
Big-mouthed little bitch. How the hell did she find out?

MAUREEN
Never mind about her—why didn't you tell me?

FLOYD
Because ah didn't want you talkin' to Dad before ah did.

MAUREEN
You mean you haven't even asked him yet?

FLOYD

No, ah haven't—anyway, that lake business is still in the planning stage. Ah got lots of things to do before ah get around to him.

MAUREEN

You better not let him know the Sickengers are in on it. He rates them somewhere below Herbert Hoover and the Kaiser.

FLOYD

Ah thought that spot was reserved for me.

MAUREEN

Sickengers, barbecues, the Genet farm, God, I wish I could get out of this town for a while.

FLOYD

Oh no, nuthin' doin'. Not another trip.

MAUREEN

Why the hell not?

FLOYD

Well, hell, didn't we go plumb all over Europe last year and took that stupid-assed cruise to the Careabeean the year before that?

MAUREEN

Caribbean!!!

FLOYD

Careabeean! Never was so sick in mah life.

MAUREEN

That's because you got drunk ever' night.

FLOYD

Damned right ah did. Ah stayed drunk in Europe too. God-

damned dirty cities, all them foreigners runnin' around
screamin' at the top of their lungs.

MAUREEN

All right, all right, so you hated it. I'm sorry I made you go.

FLOYD

Sons-a-bitchin' Limey cab drivers. No more of that by-God
Europe for me, ah can tell you that.

MAUREEN

How about goin' to Acapulco for a couple of weeks
then?

FLOYD

Hell with it. If ah want to see a bunch of Mexicans ah'll go
over to the Catholic church.

MAUREEN

Well, we're not goin' to just stay *here* all summer, are we?

FLOYD

What's wrong with that? You never used to want to run off
every summer. Lived in this town all our life, married for
about two hundred years, and all of a sudden you get the itch
to take off all over the by-God world.

MAUREEN

Well, why the hell not? God, I'd give anything to be able to
look out of a window and see somethin' else besides wind-
mills, mesquite, tumbleweeds, and the beautiful skyline of
Bradleyville.

FLOYD

We cain't go nowhere this summer, ah tell you.

MAUREEN

Why?

FLOYD
Because you and ah got work to do. Important work.

MAUREEN
I don't want anything to do with your damn land deal.

FLOYD
Ah'm not talkin' about that. Ah'm talkin' about this. *(He takes a letter out of his inside coat pocket.)*

MAUREEN
What's that?

FLOYD
This here is a letter from the Mirabeau B. Lamar Military Academy in Galveston.

MAUREEN
So what. You fixin' to join up or somethin'?

FLOYD
Now damnit, cut out the wise-assin' and pay attention.

MAUREEN
All right, all right.

FLOYD
It seems that the school is movin' from its original campus to a bran'-new location across town.

MAUREEN
Good for them.

FLOYD
Now, it just so happens that Dad is the oldest livin' graduate of this fine institution, and all them little ka-dets are gonna hold a big celebration, with him as the guest of honor.

MAUREEN
I still don't see what that's got to do with you and me.

FLOYD

After ah got this letter, ah got on the phone and explained how Dad was in a wheelchair and couldn't travel. So the commandant agreed to move the whole ceremony right here to Bradleyville.

MAUREEN

Why didn't you tell me about this before?

FLOYD

(Chuckles.) Surprised you, didn't ah?

MAUREEN

Yeah, I'm surprised all right, but not too damned overwhelmed. What's the big deal about a school full of little kids dressed in soldier suits coming to town?

FLOYD

The whole school isn't comin', jest the band and the honor guard. Besides that, the kids aren't important—it's the graduates and their wives.

MAUREEN

The graduates?

FLOYD

That's right. *(He looks at the letter.)* Two generals, three full colonels, one-two-three-four congressmen, six state senators, an ex-lieutenant governor, and a whole raft of businessmen and such like.

MAUREEN

Interesting.

FLOYD

Damn right, it's interestin'. Hell's fire! All the people who are anybody at all go to good old M. B. Lamar. Dad graduated from there in 1905 before he went on to the A&M. As it turns out, he's the only living member of the school's first graduating class. Seems that most of his classmates were killed off in the First World War.

MAUREEN
That's kind of sad.

FLOYD
What's sad about it? This is goin' to mean a helluva lot of publicity for Bradleyville. TV and newspaper people comin' down here. The commandant told me that even the *Life* magazine people are interested.

MAUREEN
Really?

FLOYD
Damn right. There'll be people comin' here from all over the state. We're going to have a banquet, a ceremony, cocktail parties, the works. Hell's fire, it's the biggest thing to hit this town in years.

MAUREEN
Yeah. Well, it will give me something to do. How much time we got?

FLOYD
The actual ceremony isn't scheduled until September, but the commandant of the school is going to be here in a couple of days to help make the arrangements.

MAUREEN
Uh-huh, you gonna get that waxy, rocky Big Spring outfit to cater the banquet?

FLOYD
Hell no. These are important people—we can't feed them no crappy barbecue. We'll have to use the country club.

MAUREEN
Oh, for Christ's sake!

FLOYD
Or the Tumbleweed Room at the Holiday Inn.

MAUREEN
They'll take one look at those plastic tulips and that damn
cattle-stampede mural and run outta there like rabbits. No,
let's go ahead and book the country club.

FLOYD
All right.

MAUREEN
Now, what about invitations?

FLOYD
Well, other than the folks comin' in, I figger to restrict it to
the country-club membership.

MAUREEN
(Sarcastically) Damn right, we don't want no riffraff showin'
up.

FLOYD
Then ah was thinkin' about a small party out here. I mean,
with the commandant's group and some of our close friends.

MAUREEN
Close friends, huh? Boy, that'll make it small all right.

FLOYD
You'll have to come up with somethin' to entertain the wives
one afternoon. Ah've been thinkin' of throwin' a stag fish fry
out to the lake.

MAUREEN
Okay. Oh, by the way, when are you going to tell the Colonel?

FLOYD
Ah thought ah'd break it to him the day before the commandant gets here. That way he'll be ready for ever'thin'.

MAUREEN
What if he says no?

FLOYD
He's not goin' to say no.

MAUREEN
Well, you know how he is. Spoze he gits it into his head that he doesn't want to be honored by dear old M. B. Lamar?

FLOYD
He will when he hears about the memorial service.

MAUREEN
Memorial service?

FLOYD
For all the fallen heroes of the academy. Seein' as how most of his classmates were killed in the war, ah figgered it couldn't miss.

MAUREEN
Memorial services, stag parties, graduates—quite a parade. You know, it occurs to me that this ceremony for the Colonel is really comin' up at a good time, isn't it?

FLOYD
What do you mean?

MAUREEN

What I mean is, isn't it lucky that you were able to talk this commandant of that military academy into coming down here with all those big shots at the very time when you and Clarence are goin' into the lake-development business?

FLOYD

(Raising his glass.) Damn right.

MAUREEN

Boy, you don't miss a trick, do you?

FLOYD

Ah do the best ah can.

MAUREEN

Well, I better get on over to the country club and get things started. Listen, I just remembered, Reverend Stone wouldn't have anythin' to do with the memorial service, would he?

FLOYD

I'm gonna get him to conduct it. He's spozed to call me some time today about it. *(MAUREEN bursts into laughter.)* *What the hell's so funny?*

(MAUREEN continues off, laughing.)

ACT I
Scene 2

The den about an hour later. FLOYD *and* MAUREEN *are gone.*
MIKE TREMAINE *opens the patio door and wheels the* COLO-
NEL *in.*

MIKE
There ain't any cars in the garage. I 'speck Mr. and Mrs.
Kinkaid have gone off some place.

COLONEL
That's fine with me. Have a little peace and quiet around
here for a while. Sit down, Mike, sit down and take it
easy.

MIKE
Well, ah should be gittin' back on that fence, Colonel.

COLONEL
Hell with it. Floyd can wait on that damned fence. Sit down
now, damnit, that's an order.

MIKE
(Sitting down.) Yes, sir.

COLONEL
You do much fishin', Mike?

MIKE
Yes, sir, ever' chance ah git.

COLONEL
Who you go fishin' with?

MIKE
George Williams, mostly.

COLONEL
Ah used to go fishin' with your daddy. Betcha didn't know that, did you?

MIKE
Yes, sir. My dad used to brag on the catfish you-all would catch.

COLONEL
Old Carter Tremaine and me used to fish all the time till mah damn legs went out on me.

MIKE
Yes, sir, ah know.

COLONEL
How is old Carter? By God, ah ain't seen him in a long spell.

MIKE
He's dead, Colonel. He passed away two years ago last winter.

COLONEL
Oh, God, that's right. Ah forgot. You know, your daddy and me was good friends. Ah'm plumb sorry, ah forgot about him passin' away.

MIKE
That's okay, Colonel.

COLONEL
Hell, old Carter and me useta have a lot of fun, damned if we didn't. By God, ah really miss goin' fishin'.

MIKE
You can come with George and me any time you want to, Colonel

COLONEL
Naw, ah'd jest git in the way.

MIKE
You wouldn't git in the way, Colonel. We could rig up a special chair in the boat.

COLONEL
Ah would too and you know it. Don't lie to me, Mike Tremaine, you ain't no good at it.

MIKE
Yes, sir.

COLONEL
Wouldn't be no fun without Carter anyway. Damn death, damn it straight to hell. Takin' things away from a feller, don't give a goddamned thing, jest takes away. Took away Carter, took away Franklin. You remember my boy Franklin, don't you, Mike?

MIKE
Yes, sir, ah sure do.

COLONEL
Killed in 1942, flyin' a B-17. Crashed in Florida on a by-God trainin' flight. Jesus, what a waste.

MIKE
Yes, sir.

COLONEL

Bumble-dickin' death. Lets a worthless old fart like me go on and buries a fine young man like Franklin in some stinkin' swamp. Ah kept havin' dreams after Franklin was killed. Dreamed that ah could see his airplane in the water and he was callin' to me to help him get out.

MIKE

(Uncomfortably) Well, Colonel, ah gotta be goin'. Ah'd shore like to git that fence done affore dark. *(He starts to door.)*

COLONEL

You and George ever fish that big cove over to mah place on the lake?

MIKE

Yes, sir. There's some nice big bass in there all right, but they're shore hard to git to.

COLONEL

Brushy, ain't it?

MIKE

Pretty brushy, yes, sir.

COLONEL

That's 'cause ah don't let anybody fool around with it. Floyd wanted to put a boathouse or somethin' in there once, but ah said, Hell, no, leave it like it is, it's better that way.

MIKE

Colonel, ah know it ain't none of mah business, but could ah ask you somethin' about that place?

COLONEL

Shore, Mike. Whattayou wanna know?

MIKE
Well, sir, it's about that spot we went out to look at. Was there a shore-enough town there once?

COLONEL
Well, no, not exactly a town. It was more like a settlement, you might say.

MIKE
A settlement?

COLONEL
That's right, way back before ah went to the Philippines. Ah was workin' here then on mah father's ranch.

MIKE
Out on the Seven Spear?

COLONEL
That's right. My father was a tough old booger. He had mah ass in the saddle from by-God dawn to dusk. Well, sir, Charlie Parsons and me was holed up in a line shack one time right out yonder where Lake Bradleyville is now, when we seen five or six wagonloads of people settin' up right across our fence line. It turns out that those folks were some kind of religious outfit that bought the land and moved out on it to form a farmin' community.

MIKE
I never heard nuthin' about that.

COLONEL
Ain't many people still around that remembers 'em. They built 'em some houses and put 'em up a great big barn that they called their community storehouse.

MIKE
What sort of religion was they?

COLONEL

Cain't remember no more, but they damn sure weren't no Baptists. By God, we really used to have some dandy dances in that barn. One of them farmers was a feller named Genet and he had two of the prettiest daughters that you ever seen.

MIKE

Looked pretty good to you boys, did they?

COLONEL

You're damned right they did. Old Charlie Parsons and ah started courtin' up with them two gals right off the bat.

MIKE

The Genet girls?

COLONEL

Marie and Suzette. They was French, you see, that's why them girls had pretty names like that. Ever' chance old Charlie and me would get, we'd ride over there and visit. God in heaven, but Suzette was a good-lookin' girl. Kindly short, you know, with blondish hair and this little tiny waist. Ah could put both hands around it just like nuthin' at all. Ah seen lots of girls, Mike. Ah seen 'em in the Philippines, ah seen 'em in Mexico. Ah seen them madam-oselles over there to France, but none of 'em, never, any place, was as by-God good-lookin' as little Suzette Genet from right out yonder on that farm. Jesus, but ah was crazy about that girl. Betcha didn't know that, did you? Was moonin' around about her one day and fell off my horse right into a stock tank.

MIKE

What happened to all them people? There ain't nuthin' out there now.

COLONEL

They went bust. Dried up. They did real good for a couple

of years, made good crops. Then we had a goddamned dry spell and it finished 'em. They hung on for a while, but the damned sun just burnt 'em out and they had to move on. Ever' family just packed up and pulled out.

MIKE
And Suzette?

COLONEL
She went with them.

MIKE
Didn't you try to stop her?

COLONEL
Shore ah did. But she said she had to go on with her folks, help set up another community some place else. Ah never seen her again, never again. After ah took up mah commission and went over to the Philippines, mah father bought up that land and had the houses knocked down. Then later on they dammed up the creek to make Lake Bradleyville. So where the farms was is all under water now. But them foundations up there on that little rise, that's where ah was a young feller in love once. That's why ah don't let anybody fool with that property. Ah like to keep it for rememberin'. That's important to an old feller like me, havin' places that stay the same for rememberin' on.

MIKE
Yes, sir, ah reckon so.

COLONEL
Now, ah don't mean to say nuthin' about Floyd and Franklin's mama. Elizabeth was a good woman. Ah jest don't remember her the same way as Suzette.

MIKE
Mrs. Kinkaid was real nice.

COLONEL

Ah don't even mind what Brewster and Floyd done to the Seven Spear, breakin' it up the way they did, drillin' oil wells, bringin' in that fat-assed stock and them damn stinkin' sheep, but, by God, ah made 'em let the Genet farm alone. Bumble-dickin' money-grubbers.

(FLOYD's voice is heard from the living room.)

FLOYD

Maureen, you home yet?

COLONEL

Oh, hell! Floyd's back.

FLOYD

(Entering den.) Oh, howdy, Dad, Mike. How was the drive?

MIKE

Pretty good, Mr. Kinkaid. We drove out to the Colonel's place out on the lake.

FLOYD

Oh, is that right? You know, ah want to talk to you about that a little later, Dad.

COLONEL

Talk about what?

FLOYD

The place on the lake.

COLONEL

What about it?

FLOYD

(Ignoring him.) You finish that fence yet, Mike?

MIKE
Well, no, sir, you see the Colonel, he . . .

FLOYD
You ain't gonna git it done sittin' around in here, Mike. Hell, now it's gone plumb dark and it still ain't done.

MIKE
Ah'll git it done tomorrow for shore.

FLOYD
That ain't gittin' it done today.

MIKE
Yes, sir.

COLONEL
Why don't you shut the hell up, Floyd! Damnit, ah told Mike to forgit that damn fence. Ah wanted to talk to him.

FLOYD
Now, Dad, ah don't want you keepin' Mike from his chores. There's too much work to do around here without you wastin' Mike's time.

COLONEL
Then why the hell don't *you* do some of it? My father made me work my butt off and you don't do a damn thing.

FLOYD
(*Patiently*) That's right, Dad. Now, Mike, before you come out here in the morning ah want you to go by the feed store and pick up some oats and tell that damn fool Milo Crawford that ah want by-God *oats* and not chicken mash.

MIKE
Yes, sir.

COLONEL

(To FLOYD*)* Git on out to the ranch and mark them damn sheep you so all-fired proud of.

MIKE

Well, ah'll be gittin' on home now, Mr. Kinkaid. So long, Colonel.

COLONEL

So long there, Mike, enjoyed the talk.

FLOYD

Don't forget them oats.

MIKE

No, sir. *(He exits out the patio door.)*

COLONEL

Damn nice boy. Ah used to go fishin' with his daddy. Betcha didn't know that, did you?

FLOYD

Shore, Dad, you told me.

COLONEL

Old Carter Tremaine. Hooked me in the ear with a plug one time.

FLOYD

Yeah, ah know.

COLONEL

Hurt like hell. Franklin was out there with us, wasn't more than six years old. Kept yellin', "Daddy's been gaffed, Daddy's been gaffed!"

FLOYD

Shore, Dad. Now, if you can be still for a second, ah need to talk to you.

COLONEL

Hell's fire! It weren't no gaff at all. It was just a little old fish hook.

FLOYD

Please, Dad, if ah could just . . .

COLONEL

(Chuckles.) "Daddy's been gaffed."

FLOYD

Dad, ah need to talk to you!

COLONEL

Well, go ahead, who's stoppin' you!

FLOYD

You are, with that damn silly story.

COLONEL

What's so damn silly about it? Mah ear was sore as hell. 'Course you don't care nuthin' about that, do you?

FLOYD

Of course ah do, it's just . . .

COLONEL

Franklin cared, he cried and cried 'cause his daddy was hurt.

FLOYD

Jesus, that happened years ago.

COLONEL

Still got the by-God scar.

FLOYD

Carter and Franklin are dead now, so forgit about it.

COLONEL

Yes, that's right. Franklin's gone now, down in that damn

swamp. My boy's gone, my good boy that cried when ah was
hurt.

FLOYD
Shore, shore.

COLONEL
They wouldn't let me see his body, you know, but ah knew,
ah knew how it looked. Ah seen a Englishman's body after
his plane crashed near our trench. He was tore all to pieces.
Ah know what it's like to fall, so ah didn't need to see Franklin, but ah knew.

FLOYD
All right, all right. Let's just forget about Franklin.

COLONEL
Cain't forgit. He keeps comin' into my mind.

FLOYD
Damnit, Dad, listen to me!

COLONEL
Who you yellin' at!

FLOYD
You, ah'm yellin' at you!

COLONEL
Where do you get off yellin' at your father! That ain't no way
for a boy to do.

FLOYD
Ah know, but . . .

COLONEL
Ah never yelled at my father. By God, he'd have beat my
butt off with a fence post.

FLOYD
Dad . . .

COLONEL
Ah'll bet Maureen said somethin' about me. Well, whatever she said ah done, ah never done it. She makes up things, that woman does, makes 'em up. She and that durn Sickenger girl.

FLOYD
Now don't start on Maureen. She takes good care of you.

COLONEL
Don't give a damn about me. Parties is all she likes; new cars, gossip, and parties. When she's not out to that damn country club, she's sittin' around makin' up stories about me.

FLOYD
Maureen ain't said nuthin' about you!

COLONEL
That's 'cause she don't like me.

FLOYD
What?

COLONEL
She never talks about me 'cause she don't like me.

FLOYD
But you just said . . .

COLONEL
What the hell we sittin' around here gassin' about Maureen for? Ah thought you wanted to ask me somethin'.

FLOYD
That's right, ah do.

COLONEL

Well, go ahead. Ah damn sure ain't goin' no place. Bumble-
dickin' wheelchair cain't even go fishin'.

FLOYD

Ah need to talk to you about the Genet farm.

COLONEL

What about it?

FLOYD

Well, Clarence Sickenger and ah were talkin' to old man
Cullers down at the bank today.

COLONEL

Heard about that. What did he beat you out of?

FLOYD

Nuthin'.

COLONEL

Don't believe it.

FLOYD

Clarence and ah are thinkin' of goin' into a little develop-
ment project.

COLONEL

You are, are you?

FLOYD

I'm gonna lay it right on the line, Dad. We wanna do somethin' with that Genet farm property.

COLONEL

The hell you say! You cain't touch that land. It's mine!

FLOYD
Now don't get all excited, Dad. Just hear me out.

COLONEL
Don't wanna hear you out. Ah told you when you took over my half of the Kinkaid properties that you could do anythin' you damn well wanted to with 'em, but you was to keep your hands off the Genet farm, ain't that right?

FLOYD
Yes, Dad, that's right.

COLONEL
Well, there you are.

FLOYD
Dad, that lake property is damn valuable.

COLONEL
No, it ain't. The only person it's valuable to is me.

FLOYD
Why, for Christ's sake? What the hell you got out there, a gold mine or somethin'?

COLONEL
Ain't none of your damned business. Ah got mah reasons for wantin' that property and that by God is enough.

FLOYD
Well, it ain't enough for me.

COLONEL
It damned well better be.

FLOYD
Listen, Dad, Clarence has been in touch with an architect in Dallas. They've got an idea for sectionin' off that land into

two-acre plots. Jesus, with his property and the Genet farm joined together, Clarence and ah will own the whole north side of the lake.

COLONEL
Who the hell would want a two-acre plot?

FLOYD
Lots of people.

COLONEL
What the hell for? Nobody in the world could make a livin' farmin' on two acres. Unless it's one of them damn Chinamen or somethin'.

FLOYD
It ain't for farmin'.

COLONEL
Bringin' in the Chinamen, that's what you're aimin' to do! The by-God yeller peril! Right here, right here in Bradley-ville!

FLOYD
Oh, for Christ's sake.

COLONEL
I'll fight it. Just see if ah don't. I'll round up mah lodge broth-ers. By God, we'll fortify the land with trenches and bobwire. Shoot the yeller backside off ever' goddamned Chinaman you bring around here.

FLOYD
We ain't bringin' in any Chinamen, damnit! These are goin' to be exclusive summer homes.

COLONEL
Summer homes?

FLOYD
That's right. Jesus, we could make a fortune.

COLONEL
You got enough money now.

FLOYD
We could dredge out the cove and put in the biggest damn marina you ever seen.

COLONEL
You cain't have the Genet farm.

FLOYD
We're goin' to call it Mumford County Estates. Nine-hole golf course, water-skiin', skeet shootin', horseback ridin', private club—the works.

COLONEL
Mumford County Estates. Who came up with that one?

FLOYD
Clarence.

COLONEL
That figures. Ah recollect as how them Sickengers is related to old Governor Mumford.

FLOYD
Ah don't know if they are or not. Now . . .

COLONEL
Why, they named this county after old Governor Mumford is beyond me. Should have named it Kinkaid County.

FLOYD
Sure, Dad, now . . .

COLONEL

Ah'm proud to be from Texas, ah'm proud to be from Bradleyville, but by God ah'm not a damned bit proud to be from
Mumford County.

FLOYD

All right, all right, so it's a stupid name.

COLONEL

(Chuckles.) How would you like to walk up to some feller and
have to say, "Howdy, ah'm Clarence Sickenger and ah'm
from Mumford County."

FLOYD

Damnit, Dad, what about the project?

COLONEL

What project?

FLOYD

The lake project.

COLONEL

Frilly, sad-assed waste of time. Ruin the land puttin' up a
by-God carnival.

FLOYD

We'll have folks movin' in here from all over the country.

COLONEL

Don't graze the land, don't work the land, don't do a damned
thing but throw beer bottles and little pieces of paper all over
it.

FLOYD

Not if you control it. You make it exclusive and control it.

COLONEL

Best way to control crap like that is not to let it happen at all.

FLOYD

Dad, ah need that land. Clarence is goin' over to Dallas to see the architect again. Hell's fire, we wanna git started on this thing.

COLONEL

You cain't have the Genet farm.

FLOYD

It jest beats the hell out of me why you hang on to that property. For God's sake, *you* ain't growin' or grazin' anything out there. The damn land's just goin' to seed.

COLONEL

That's all right if it does. The Genet farm is mine and by God it's gonna stay just like it is.

FLOYD

If you would just listen for a second.

COLONEL

Tired of listening. You cain't have that land, that is an *order* and that is a *fact!*

FLOYD

Like tryin' to talk to a damned brick wall!

MAUREEN

(Appearing at the door) Shore is nice to be home again, you miss all this shoutin' and yellin' out in the big wide world.

FLOYD

You stay outta this!

MAUREEN
Outta what? Hell, I just got here.

COLONEL
Ah don't wanna talk no more. Ah'm tired. Ah wanna go to mah room.

MAUREEN
Let me help you, Colonel.

COLONEL
Git away, ah kin run this thing all by mahself! *(He wheels into his room.)*

MAUREEN
Ah'll have Ida Ruth bring in your supper after a bit.

COLONEL
(Offstage) Don't want no supper. Damnit, leave me alone!

MAUREEN
What's got him so riled up tonight?

FLOYD
Hell, ah don't know, he's been on the peck all afternoon.

MAUREEN
Uh-huh. You-all wouldn't have been discussin' the lake-development plan by any chance?

FLOYD
We might have mentioned it once or twice.

MAUREEN
Trust Clarence to come up with a dimwitted name like Mumford County Estates.

FLOYD
There ain't nuthin' set yet. It's jest an idea.

MAUREEN
An idea that the Colonel obviously didn't take too kindly to.

FLOYD
He'll come around. He never likes anythin' the first time he hears it.

MAUREEN
You really think it's a good idea, Floyd? I mean, let's face it, Lake Bradleyville isn't exactly my idea of the fun spot of the Southwest. All that's out there are some old boat docks and a bait stand run by somebody named Bowdwin Cassidy.

FLOYD
That's why it's so perfect. Hell's fire, that's a big lake out there, and it's practically untouched. The way Clarence and ah got it figgered is that we'll cater only to money people, big-money people. Mumford County Estates is goin' to be exclusive, baby. Rich and exclusive.

MAUREEN
Rich and exclusive. Well, there it is—the Bradleyville Country Club motto. The whole hollow useless thing all over again. A lake full of rich and exclusive, sag-bellied, loud-mouthed bores—water skis, bass boats, Chris-Crafts, everything that "rich and exclusive" can buy.

FLOYD
You're damn right they're goin' to buy— What's wrong with that? The way it is now, that damn land out there is just goin' to waste. This way the Colonel gets his ceremony, you get your picture in *Life* magazine, and old Floyd kicks off a million-dollar deal. It's a perfect plan.

MAUREEN
Perfect except for one thing.

COLONEL
(Calling from offstage) Damnit to hell, where's mah supper! You-all expect me to starve to death out here!

MAUREEN
Him.

ACT II
Scene 1

The den, four days later.
As the scene opens, the COLONEL *is onstage asleep in his wheelchair. He is dressed in Western-cut pants, slippers, and his old World War I officer's tunic.)*

MAUREEN
(Offstage) Ida Ruth, make sure there's enough ice, ah've already checked the bar. (*She enters the room and gently shakes the* COLONEL.) Colonel, Colonel—wake up.

COLONEL
Is it my turn on guard again? Hell's fire, ah jest turned in.

MAUREEN
Colonel, wake up!

COLONEL
What . . . who . . . what the hell you want?

MAUREEN
Time to wake up, Colonel. Floyd and Major Ketchum will be here any minute.

COLONEL
Major who?

MAUREEN
Major Ketchum. The commandant of the military school.

COLONEL
Never heard of him.

MAUREEN
Of course you've heard of him, Colonel. My God, Floyd spent
all day yesterday explainin' ever'thin' to you. That's why you
put on your uniform, remember?

COLONEL
Oh, yeah, ah remember now. Ah'm the oldest living graduate
of some damn thing.

MAUREEN
That's right, Colonel.

COLONEL
Outlived ever' damn one of 'em. Betcha didn't know that,
did you?

MAUREEN
Of course I know that, Colonel.

COLONEL
Ever' damn one of 'em!

MAUREEN
That's right, Colonel.

COLONEL
Probably don't sound like much, but then you ain't never
done it, have you?

MAUREEN
No, Colonel, I haven't.

COLONEL
That's 'cause you ain't old enough. How old are you anyway?

MAUREEN
I'm forty-two years old.

COLONEL
Well, you ain't as old as ah am, but you're gittin' there, ain't you, kid?

MAUREEN
Faster than you think.

COLONEL
That's 'cause you don't take proper care of yourself. Did you check your feet today?

MAUREEN
My feet?

COLONEL
Yes, damnit, your feet! Proper foot hygiene will save your life one of these days.

MAUREEN
Ah'll remember that the next time ah go over the top.

COLONEL
Always had my men check their feet.

MAUREEN
Good for you.

COLONEL
Who was it you said was comin' to see me?

MAUREEN
Major Ketchum, the commandant of the military school.

COLONEL

Wonder how come the commandant ain't nuthin' but a little old piddly-butted major?

MAUREEN

I wouldn't know.

COLONEL

We had a general for a commandant when ah was there.

MAUREEN

Is that a fact?

COLONEL

Yep. An ex-Confederate general.

MAUREEN

One of old Robert's boys, right?

COLONEL

Who?

MAUREEN

Robert E. Lee.

COLONEL

Hell no! It weren't Robert E. Lee. What would Robert E. Lee be doin' runnin' a little old South Texas military school? My God, girl, use your head.

MAUREEN

I didn't say that!

COLONEL

That would be like puttin' old Black Jack Pershing in charge of a national-guard armory or some damn thing.

MAUREEN

What I meant was . . .

COLONEL

'Course ah wouldn't put it past 'em. Bumble-dickin' gover'-ment dumb butts. Treated us doughboys like dirt after we got home. Cut off all the goddamned whiskey and took away all the jobs. Whipped the Hun for 'em and they turned on us.

MAUREEN

Shore, Colonel, shore.

COLONEL

President Wilson's wife was runnin' the by-God country. Betcha didn't know that, did you?

MAUREEN

Well, no, ah . . .

COLONEL

Women votin', women runnin' for office. Wigglin' their fat cans around in the votin' booth.

MAUREEN

Most of the fat cans ah've seen around the old votin' booth were wearin' Levi's.

COLONEL

What the hell's that spozed to mean!

(*Voices are heard offstage; then* FLOYD *appears at the door.*)

FLOYD

Well, here we are! Dad, ah'd like you to meet Major LeRoy W. Ketchum.

(MAJOR KETCHUM *marches into the room, followed by* CA-DET WHOPPER TURNBULL. *The* MAJOR *is a portly gentleman wearing a uniform that is closely akin to a World War II Army Air Corps officer's "pinks." On his right shoulder is a large patch with the Lone Star flag and the letters*

M.B.L.M.A. over it. CADET TURNBULL *is a very military-looking lad of seventeen. His uniform is much like the* MA-JOR*'s, only he wears large West Point-type sergeant's chevrons and shiny black riding boots.)*

KETCHUM
Colonel J. C. Kinkaid, this is indeed a pleasure, sir! *(He pumps the* COLONEL*'s hand.)*

COLONEL
Yeah, glad to know you.

FLOYD
This is my wife, Maureen.

MAUREEN
Glad to meet you.

KETCHUM
My pleasure, ma'am. Yes, indeed, my pleasure.

COLONEL
Ever'thin's a pleasure to this feller.

KETCHUM
Colonel, Mrs. Kinkaid, I'd like you to meet one of our boys. Cadet Adjutant Whopper Turnbull.

WHOPPER
(Whipping out a salute.) Glad to meet you, Colonel. Mrs. Kinkaid, ma'am.

COLONEL
God Almighty, damn! Did you see him whip out that salute, Floyd? You sure can zip it out there, boy.

WHOPPER
Thank you, sir.

KETCHUM
Cadet Sergeant Turnbull here is one of our most promising men, Colonel. A real product of Mirabeau B. Lamar.

COLONEL
Damn fine-looking soldier.

WHOPPER
Thank you, sir.

MAUREEN
Well, you-all got business to talk over, so I'll just toddle on out.

KETCHUM
A real pleasure, ma'am.

MAUREEN
I know. *(She exits.)*

COLONEL
How come you wearin' them boots, boy? They bringin' back the horse cavalry?

WHOPPER
No, sir, these are standard dress-uniform requirements at Mirabeau B. Lamar, sir.

KETCHUM
We feel that it gives the boys pride and military bearing.

COLONEL
Ah served in the cavalry with old Black Jack Pershing back in 1916. Betcha didn't know that, did you?

WHOPPER
Yes, sir. I've done an in-depth study of your military career, Colonel.

COLONEL

Old Black Jack. There was a general for you. Ever' inch a soldier. Ah remember once when we was chasin' that fat little greaser Pancho Villa down there in Mexico. Well, sir, ah was havin' a cup of coffee in the officers' mess. Hot as hell that day and the wind was blowin' the tent sides back and forth. Flap, flap, flap.

FLOYD

Sure, sure. Now, Dad, ah think we should go over the agenda.

KETCHUM

Cadet Turnbull, the agenda.

WHOPPER

Yes, sir. *(He places a small black case on the desk and snaps it open.)*

COLONEL

Cavalry wasn't any damn good over there in France though. The machine guns saw to that. Used horses to pull wagons and artillery and such like, but no by-God cavalry charges.

KETCHUM

(Taking a paper from WHOPPER.*)* Now, Colonel, starting at . . .

COLONEL

Ah was there when a horse-drawn ammunition convoy was shelled once. Jesus, what a mess.

FLOYD

Dad, Major Ketchum is . . .

COLONEL

Them poor horses, them poor, poor horses. Blowed apart right in the traces. Ah seen one with his back broke tryin' to pull himself along with his two front legs and cryin' like a baby.

FLOYD
Damnit, Dad! Come to, will you!

COLONEL
Another one had its stomach shot out and was runnin' around in little circles screamin' and steppin' on its own guts.

WHOPPER
My God!

KETCHUM
Easy there, Cadet Turnbull. Now, Colonel, we've all seen our share of war's hell, but now we must bend our attention to the affair at hand.

COLONEL
Git out of the cavalry, son. You ain't got a chance against heavy artillery and machine guns.

KETCHUM
(To FLOYD*)* Mr. Kinkaid, could you please get the Colonel to attend to this matter?

FLOYD
Damnit, Dad, pay attention!

COLONEL
To what? You ain't said nuthin' yet. Foolin' around here, wastin' mah time. Ah got a lodge meetin' to go to this evenin'. Git on with it, Ketchup. That is a by-God order!

KETCHUM
Right, Colonel Kinkaid. Now, according to your son here, the best site for the ceremony is at the Bradleyville Country Club.

FLOYD
Yes, that's right.

COLONEL
Yeah, well, what the hell.

KETCHUM
We will have the cadet band here, of course. They will open
the proceedings with the national anthem, followed by "The
Spirit of Mirabeau B. Lamar," and then a rousing rendition
of "Dixie." I will then introduce Captain Scott, my adjutant,
who will call the roll of the class of 1905. After the first five
names are called, "Taps" will be played. Then, Colonel Kinkaid will be introduced. His chair will be wheeled up to the
speakers' stand by Cadet Adjutant Turnbull and escorted by
picked members of the honor guard. The band will play
"Over There."

COLONEL
Don't like that damned song. *"Yanks* are comin'," for
Christ's sake. We were by-God *doughboys,* not *Yanks.* Call
a Texas boy a *Yank* over there and you were lookin' to have
a Springfield bashed over your head.

KETCHUM
Well, of course, Colonel, we'll play any song you want.

COLONEL
Know how we used to sing that song? "We'll be over, we're
coming over, but we won't come back, we'll be buried over
there." That's how we used to sing it.

KETCHUM
What song do you want, Colonel?

COLONEL
How about "The Old Gray Mare." That's what we sang when
we crossed the Marne in 1918.

KETCHUM
Somehow I don't think that would be, uh, hardly appropri-
ate.

COLONEL
(Singing) "Would you rather be a colonel with an eagle on your shoulder or a private with a chicken on his knee?" *(Laughs; singing)* "Mademoiselle from Armenteers, parley-voo, Mademoiselle from Armenteers, parley-voo, Mademoiselle from Armenteers, hasn't been *(He whistles and gives the thumbs-up sign.)* in forty years, Hinky, dinky, parley-voo." *(To* WHOPPER*)* How do you like that one, sonny?

WHOPPER
Well, I, uh . . .

COLONEL
You can sing that one to the boys in your barracks, they'll git a kick out of it.

WHOPPER
Yeah, uh, sure.

FLOYD
What about "The Eyes of Texas"?

KETCHUM
Excellent suggestion.

COLONEL
(Singing) "There's a long, long nail a-stickin' into the sole of my shoe."

KETCHUM
Yes, very funny, Colonel. Now, after the Colonel has been wheeled into place, I will introduce the rest of our honored graduates.

COLONEL
Who are they?

KETCHUM
Cadet Turnbull. List.

WHOPPER
Yes, sir. *(He snaps a paper out of the case and hands it to* KETCHUM.*)*

KETCHUM
Let's see. Two generals, three full colonels, four congress-men, six state senators, an ex-lieutenant governor . . .

COLONEL
All them fellers graduated from Mirabeau B. Lamar?

KETCHUM
That's correct, Colonel.

COLONEL
Jesus, makes my old class of 1905 seem kindly piddlin', don't it?

KETCHUM
Why, of course not, Colonel.

COLONEL
But then again, most of us is dead, ain't we?

KETCHUM
Yes, well, uh. You know, we've not only produced many gallant soldiers and public servants at Mirabeau B. Lamar but several prominent Texas businessmen as well.

COLONEL
Money people, huh. See there, Floyd, now you'll have some-body to talk to. Floyd here is a big plan maker. Summer-home magnate. Ain't that right, Floyd?

FLOYD
Let's not get started on that, Dad. Go ahead, Major.

KETCHUM
After I finish the list of honored graduates, then Cadet Turn-bull will give a synopsis of Colonel Kinkaid's career.

COLONEL
Well, good for you, sonny.

WHOPPER
Thank you, sir.

COLONEL
When do ah git to say somethin'?

FLOYD
You don't, Dad.

COLONEL
Why the hell not?

FLOYD
It's just not on the agenda, that's all.

COLONEL
Ah wanna talk about bein' down in Mexico with old Black
Jack.

FLOYD
That's what we're afraid of.

COLONEL
What the hell's that spozed to mean? Ah'll by-God say somethin' if ah want to. Who the hell's the oldest livin' graduate
around here, me or you?

FLOYD
Well, you are, but . . .

COLONEL
Damn right ah am. Oldest living graduate. You got a list of
the other fellers there, sonny boy?

WHOPPER
Other fellers?

COLONEL
Who the hell did ah outlive, anyway?

KETCHUM
You mean you don't know?

COLONEL
Can't remember exactly. Ah kindly recollect one fat kid named Tom something that we called Butter Butt. He on the list?

KETCHUM
Read the list, Cadet Turnbull.

WHOPPER
Yes, sir. *(He begins to read.) Captain Hobart A. Lowery.* Killeen, Texas. U.S.M.C.

COLONEL
Hobart A. Lowery, why sure, old Hobie. Ah remember him.

WHOPPER
Killed in action, June 25, 1918, at Belleau Wood.

COLONEL
Killed?

WHOPPER
Colonel Sidney L. Womack. Austin, Texas. U.S. Army.

COLONEL
What was that name again?

WHOPPER
Sidney L. Womack.

COLONEL
Naw. Cain't remember him.

WHOPPER
Killed in action, July 18, 1918, at Verzy.

COLONEL
Cain't remember.

WHOPPER
Captain Thomas R. Miller. Waco, Texas. U.S. Army.

COLONEL
Wait a minute, wait a minute, that's him. Tom Miller, old
Butter Butt. That's the guy, Tom Miller!

WHOPPER
Killed in action, September 12, 1918, Saint-Mihiel.

COLONEL
Saint-Mihiel. Ah was there too.

FLOYD
Listen, Dad, we don't need to hear no more. Let's git to
somethin' else.

COLONEL
No, no, ah wanna hear. Go on, sonny, read the rest of the list.

WHOPPER
Colonel Leonard H. Campbell. San Antonio, Texas. U.S.
Army.

COLONEL
Len Campbell, sure.

WHOPPER
Died April 7, 1950, in Albuquerque, New Mexico, Veterans

Hospital, of lung damage caused by mustard-gas fumes sustained in the Argonne Forest offensive, September 1918.

COLONEL
(Shaking his head.) Jesus Christ. Poor old Len.

WHOPPER
Dr. Quinton Tillery. Pampa, Texas.

COLONEL
Poor, poor old Len.

WHOPPER
Civilian doctor killed by the Japanese in Manila, 1942.

COLONEL
Hobie, Butter Butt, Len Campbell. Lemme see that list. *(He grabs it from* WHOPPER*'s hand and squints at it.)* Sidney Womack, no, ah cain't remember. Quinton Tillery, Quinton Tillery, jest cain't seem to git him. *(To* KETCHUM*)* You got a picture or somethin'?

KETCHUM
No, Colonel, I'm sorry. We had a fire at the school in 1939 that destroyed all our old photographs.

COLONEL
Cain't seem to recall those fellas.

FLOYD
Yeah, well, that's a shame, Dad. Now just listen to the memorial service that we got planned.

COLONEL
Ah'm all that's left of when we was boys. Boys like this young feller here. How's come you never told me about this affore, why didn't ah know affore that ah was the only one left?

FLOYD
You did know, Dad. Damnit, I explained ever'thin' to you a hunred times!

COLONEL
Yeah, but hell, this is different. This is a whole lot different.

FLOYD
It doesn't matter, Dad.

COLONEL
The hell it don't! Accordin' to this-here piece of paper Len Campbell was in a damned V.A. hospital for over thirty years and ah never knowed it.

KETCHUM
If you had inquired at the school, Colonel, we would have been glad to tell you of his whereabouts.

COLONEL
Just let ever'thin' slip by. Let it all slip by.

FLOYD
Dad, Dad, listen, now you can make up for it. Those men's relatives will want to see you—talk to you about when you-all were boys.

COLONEL
Hobie Lowery and Tom Miller killed over there in France. That means that they're still there, that's right, in that big American cemetery there at Verdun. Couldn't bring them boys back in them days, left 'em over there. American boys that had never been nowhere affore wind up in a goddamned coffin in France. The army just marched off and left 'em there, under all them damn white crosses. I seen 'em when Elizabeth and ah went back to France in nineteen and thirty.

We went out to Verdun and seen all them crosses. So many of 'em that they blurred into zigzaggy lines when you drove past. It was rainin' the day we got there and the cemetery was empty 'cept for me and Elizabeth and all them boys gone West. Ah walked around in the rain and felt the damnedest sorrow in mah heart that ah've ever known and ah commenced to cry. That's right. Just stood there among all them crosses and cried. Cried because of Missouri and Ohio and Texas and Pennsylvania and all of 'em—all the cities and towns and states them boys would never see again 'cause they was machine-gunned, gassed, and blowed apart, makin' the by-God world safe for democracy. *(To* WHOPPER*)* Betcha didn't know that, did you, boy?

WHOPPER
Yes, sir, I read that in . . .

COLONEL
Hell, yes, safe for democracy! Whatever in the blue-balled wonder that is. But whatever it is we done it—done the hell out of it. Ah went over to Fort Douaumont and the damn frogs was sellin' souvenirs; that's right, souvenirs. Jesus God, ain't that the way of things? Pull a feller's bacon out of the fire and he turns around and sells the drippings. They had 'em a little stand there with rusty old helmets and canteens and pieces of bobwire. Probably was sellin' skulls and finger bones out the back door—wouldn't put it past 'em one little bit. Feller that was with me that day, American feller too, paid twenty-five dollars for a busted old Enfield rifle. Told me he wanted a memento of how it musta been during the fightin' there. Ah told him to stick that Enfield up his butt sideways and march barefooted on the stickery side of the street durin' the Armistice Day parade and that would really give him an idea of how it was.

KETCHUM
Now, now, Colonel, I don't think you're taking a very military attitude about all this.

COLONEL

Go to hell with your goddamned military attitude! You weren't there, damnit!

FLOYD

Dad. Please.

KETCHUM

Now, now, Colonel, we need to think about our little ceremony.

COLONEL

To hell with it! Git your ass out of here and take your by-God oldest living graduate outfit with you. Ah don't want it, don't want no part of it. Not worth it. Not worth a bumble-dickin', goddamned thing! It ain't no honor to be the oldest livin' *anything*. Oldest living *graduate*, oldest living *Indian*, oldest living *armadillo*, oldest living *nuthin'*, 'cause that means that you're all alone! Stand around lookin' at the next-oldest livin' whippersnapper and wonder where the hell ever'body went.

FLOYD

Now listen, Dad, you're not backin' outta this. We're havin' this ceremony and you're going to be there or I'll by God know the reason why!

COLONEL

The reason why? The reason why is 'cause ah flat-assed don't want to and what's more ah ain't goin' to!

FLOYD

You damn sure are!

KETCHUM

I don't think there's any reason to prolong this, Mr. Kinkaid. It's rather obvious that the Colonel isn't going to be interested in our project.

FLOYD
Yes, he is, he really is. He's going to be with us, Major, ah guarantee it.

COLONEL
Damn sure won't and ah guarantee that!!

KETCHUM
Well, that's about it, Mr. Kinkaid. I think Cadet Turnbull and I had better be going now. Thanks for the hospitality, and if you're ever down in Galveston, look us up, will you? Colonel Kinkaid— *(He snaps a salute.)* my compliments, sir.

FLOYD
Wait a minute, Ketchum, now we made a deal.

KETCHUM
Without the Colonel there can be no deal. I have my position to think of. I can't bring all my people down here to Bradleyville to honor a man that isn't even going to attend the ceremony. No, the festivities will be held in Galveston as originally planned, I think. Well, it's certainly been a pleasure, Mr. Kinkaid, and be sure and say goodbye to your lovely wife. Come along, Cadet Turnbull. *(He and* WHOPPER *exit.)*

FLOYD
Now wait a minute, Ketchum. Look here, look here. *(He takes some papers off the desk.)* We got us all these plans, fish fry out to the lake, cocktail parties. *(He follows* KETCHUM *out the door.)* Ketchum, wait a minute. *(There is a pause while the* COLONEL *sits alone in this chair. After a bit* FLOYD *returns and leans against the door, the papers crushed in his hand.)* Well, you did it, didn't you? You messed up the whole damn thing for me.

COLONEL
What the hell did it have to do with you? It's none of your damned business if ah don't want to go to that ceremony.

FLOYD

Oh yes, it is, that's exactly what it is—*business!*

COLONEL

Ah don't know what you're talkin' about. Ah wanna go to mah lodge meeting.

FLOYD

I'll tell you what I'm talkin' about. Those people that were comin' down here. Those people that you jest told to get the hell out were important to me. Important to the lake project deal!

COLONEL

The lake project?

FLOYD

Yes, the lake project!

COLONEL

But that land's mine, ah told you, you couldn't have it.

FLOYD

Quit tellin' me what ah can and can't have. Ah've looked after this family for seventeen years, seventeen years! Me, damnit, not you. Now, by God, from now on, what ah say goes. The lake project, the military-school deal, ever'thing! From now on ah'm tellin' you what's by God what. *That*, Colonel, *that* is an order and *that* is a fact!

COLONEL

Mind your tongue, boy, you just mind your tongue. Franklin never talked that way to me.

FLOYD

To hell with Franklin. I'm sick of hearin' about him. You've stuck him down my throat ever since we were boys. Your precious goddamned Franklin. You know what

Franklin was, you really want to know? He was a stuck-up, smarty-assed twirp! My beloved big brother. My first day in high school he sicked some of his buddies on me and they took my pants off in front of the whole school. I was layin' there in the dirt, too goddamned ashamed to move, and he was laffin', laffin' louder than all the rest. I hated his guts and you put him on a pedestal forty feet high. Franklin the star! Football, basketball, track, baseball. "The Bradleyville Flash," isn't that what ever'body called him? You wanna know somethin' else? When old "Flash" bought it in that B-17, ah was happy as hell, because ah knew that if he lived out the war and came home some kind of hero I could kiss my life goodbye.

COLONEL
Ah always tried to be fair to you, Floyd.

FLOYD
Fair? You mean fair like you was today?

COLONEL
That had to do with mah life, not yours. That had to do with me and things ah cain't ever go back to and things ah forgot to do.

FLOYD
What have I asked you to do that's so damn difficult?! What the hell's so terrible about bein' honored by your old school in your own hometown?

COLONEL
Honor? What honor? What the hell kind of honor is there in a world where a boy can dishonor his dead brother and try to shame his own father?

FLOYD
I . . . oh, Jesus, Dad, I . . . I've gotta git out of here. (*He turns and exits through the patio door.*)

COLONEL
Floyd, Floyd, ah'm gonna be late for mah lodge meetin',
Floyd!

MAUREEN
*(Entering from the living room with two glasses in her
hand.)* Here, Colonel, I brought you a drink.

COLONEL
Whiskey?

MAUREEN
Whiskey.

COLONEL
Ah don't like whiskey.

MAUREEN
(Sipping from both glasses.) Suit yourself.

COLONEL
Floyd's kindly mad at me.

MAUREEN
Yeah, I heard the whole thing from the kitchen.

COLONEL
What was you doin' in the kitchen?

MAUREEN
Boozin' it up a little.

COLONEL
(Chuckling.) Knockin' back a few, were you?

MAUREEN
A few. You know, Colonel, I don't blame you one little
bit.

COLONEL
Whattayou mean?

MAUREEN
I wouldn't wanna be the bumble-dickin' oldest livin' graduate either.

COLONEL
That ain't no way for a lady to talk.

MAUREEN
Hell with it. Ah'm a member of this by-God family, ain't I?
I'll talk any way I want to.

COLONEL
Yeah, well, go ahead. Ah don't guess it matters.

MAUREEN
Hey, Colonel, cheer up. Hell, the world ain't come to an end.
And even if it has, you can bet your boots Bradleyville will
be the last place to find out.

COLONEL
It's mortifyin' to have your boy git on you like that. It ain't
natural and it's downright mortifyin'.

MAUREEN
Well, why not let him have what he wants?

COLONEL
No! No, damnit. Ah said ah wasn't goin' to that goddamned
ceremony and ah meant it.

MAUREEN
Oh, I don't mean that rooty-tooty boys'-school baloney. Floyd
deserved that. He played it about halfway crooked and got

stung on the deal. I even let myself get dumb ideas about it. No, what I'm talkin' about is your lake property.

COLONEL
He can't have the Genet farm.

MAUREEN
Why not?

COLONEL
'Cause it's mine, it's mine and ah want to keep it. There's things about it that ah remember from the old times . . . things ah used to love.

MAUREEN
Love. There's a word that hasn't been used around here in quite a while.

COLONEL
You jest don't understand.

MAUREEN
Sure, I understand, Colonel, but you've got to understand about Floyd. He needs that land b'cause he needs this project to keep goin'.

COLONEL
Ah don't know what you're talkin' about.

MAUREEN
My God, Colonel, look at him, look at us rattlin' around in this big old house with no purpose in life at all. The Kinkaid interests run themselves. Floyd's foremen and managers do all the work, and he just drives around and looks at things, or he sits around that damn country club and bets on the ball games. He needs the deals he's gonna make to keep from

goin' nuts, the houses and boat docks he's gonna build and all that big-business hokey-pokey, under-the-table baloney, and it's up to you to give it to him.

COLONEL
Gave away ever'thin', ever'thin' but the Genet farm. Now ah'm damned if ever'body doesn't want that.

MAUREEN
Not *ever'body*, Colonel.

COLONEL
Where's Floyd? Ah wanna go to mah lodge meeting.

MAUREEN
Let him have it, Colonel. Let him have that damned land!!

(The door opens and FLOYD *appears.)*

FLOYD
What's goin' on in here?

MAUREEN
Nuthin', Floyd, absolutely nuthin' at all.

COLONEL
Ah'm gonna be late for mah meetin'!

MAUREEN
Come on, Colonel, I'll drive you into town.

FLOYD
No, no, never mind, ah'll do it.

COLONEL
About by-God time. Ah wanna shuffle some dominoes.

FLOYD
Yeah, yeah, fine. Ah'll get you right into town. *(He pushes the* COLONEL *out the patio door.)*

COLONEL
Be careful what you're doin' there, damnit, you're not pushin' a bale of alfalfa.

ACT II

Scene 2

About an hour later. CLARENCE, MARTHA ANN, *and* MAUREEN *are seated in the den.*

MARTHA ANN
Why, it's jest the most excitin' little old thing ah ever heard of. Jest think, a real resort area right here in little old Bradleyville. And Clarence and Floyd are gonna run the whole thing. Why, Clarence here says that we're jest goin' to make lots of money, ain't that right, honey?

CLARENCE
That's right.

MARTHA ANN
All them houses right out there to Lake Bradleyville—jest imagine.

CLARENCE
How did Floyd's meetin' go with Major What's-his-name?

MAUREEN
Oh, it was somethin' else. But then we better wait till Floyd gets home to tell you about it.

MARTHA ANN
Ah think it's real nice how Floyd gives up his own time to take his daddy to the lodge meetin's.

MAUREEN
Yeah, he's crazy about it.

CLARENCE
Gittin' all them big shots here to Bradleyville could be one hell of a kickoff for Mumford County Estates. Ah suppose Floyd told you about that.

MAUREEN
In depth, Clarence.

MARTHA ANN
When Clarence told me about all these excitin' new plans, why, ah could jest hardly believe it. Ah mean, the Colonel havin' that little old ceremony and givin' Floyd his lake property and all that. Why, mah goodness, that's where his spooky little town is, ain't it?

MAUREEN
The very spot.

MARTHA ANN
See there, Clarence, ah told you so.

CLARENCE
Hell, there ain't no damned town out there on that property. Jest two or three broken-down foundations.

MAUREEN
How do you know?

CLARENCE
Ah went out there for a look-see.

MAUREEN
You mean you got outta your car and actually walked around out there? Ah mean, right on the ground and all?

CLARENCE
Well, hell, yes. How else would ah have seen 'em?

MAUREEN

Ah jest cain't picture you walkin' around anywhere, Clarence, gittin' your boots dusty and all that. Ah mean, you're the only guy I know that plays nine holes of golf and never gets out of his cart, like some weird kind of polo.

CLARENCE

Come off it, Maureen. Ah git plenty of exercise. Ah'm in pretty good shape for a fella mah age.

MARTHA ANN

He shore is. Clarence does his exercises ever' mornin'. He even rodeos ever' now and then, don't you, honey?

MAUREEN

I saw him last Fourth of July. He was the only member of the sheriff's posse that was mounted on a Clydesdale.

(MARTHA ANN *giggles.*)

CLARENCE

What the hell *you* laughin' at?

MARTHA ANN

"On a Clydesdale"—don't you git it?

CLARENCE

Yeah, ah git it.

MARTHA ANN

A Clydesdale is one of those great old big plow horses.

CLARENCE

Damnit, ah said ah got it! Now let it go, will you?

MARTHA ANN

Then why didn't you laugh?

CLARENCE
Because ah didn't think it was funny.

MARTHA ANN
Don't mind him, Maureen. He's jest grouchy about his old Mumford deal.

CLARENCE
You're damned right ah am. Ah'm ready to go on it and ah still don't know what Floyd's done.

MAUREEN
Ah said he'd tell you when he got home.

CLARENCE
Well, ah wish he'd hurry up. Ah'm sick of waitin' around on him.

MAUREEN
Don't you like the company, Clarence?

CLARENCE
Some of it's all right.

(FLOYD's voice comes from the living room.)

FLOYD
Hello. Ah'm back.

MAUREEN
We're in the den, Floyd.

FLOYD
(Appearing at the door.) Yeah, well, this figgers. Ah think ah'm gonna rent that damn livin' room out to boarders.

MAUREEN
Where've you been? It doesn't usually take you this long jest to drive into town and back.

FLOYD

Busted a damn fan belt. It's lucky ah was right there by the Texaco station or ah wouldn't be back yet.

CLARENCE

How did that military-school thing go today?

FLOYD

Well, now—uh. Ah need to talk to you about that, Clarence.

CLARENCE

That's why ah'm here.

FLOYD

We got troubles.

CLARENCE

What kind of troubles?

FLOYD

Dad won't go for it. He flat refuses to have anythin' to do with it.

CLARENCE

So that means all them people ain't comin' to Bradleyville, right?

FLOYD

That's about it.

CLARENCE

Uh-huh. They still gonna have the ceremony?

FLOYD

Yes. In Galveston.

CLARENCE

Okay, we'll go down there.

FLOYD
What?

CLARENCE
You still got a foot in the door. Go to Galveston, present the Colonel's regrets, and take the bows for him. Ah had some sketches made up of Mumford County Estates when ah was in Dallas. We'll take them along, corner those boys down there, and do some business with them.

MAUREEN
My God, Clarence, that's almost smart. I'm surprised at you.

MARTHA ANN
(Hugging CLARENCE.*)* Ain't he somethin' else now.

CLARENCE
Git off mah neck, will you?

FLOYD
By God, Clarence, we'll do it! Damned fine idea.

MARTHA ANN
(Kissing at CLARENCE.*)* Smart as a whip.

CLARENCE
Will you git away!

MARTHA ANN
Ah jest wanted to give you a little kiss, that's all.

CLARENCE
Well, do it later. Ah'm busy now.

MARTHA ANN
Oh, naughty you. Did you hear that, Maureen?

MAUREEN
Yeah, ah heard it. Cut out the dirty talk, will you, Clarence!

CLARENCE
What dirty talk? Ah never said nuthin'.

MARTHA ANN
He said "later," Floyd. *(Suggestively)* You know what that
means, don't you?

FLOYD
No.

MARTHA ANN
Oh, you do too.

CLARENCE
Martha Ann, will you please shut up!

MARTHA ANN
(Gesturing toward her mouth.) Tick-a-lock.

CLARENCE
That's better. Now, Floyd, what about that land of the Colonel's?

FLOYD
(Glancing at MAUREEN.*)* Well, uh, ah may have some good
news for us on that, Clarence. Ah had a long talk with Dad
about it, and ah think he's goin' to come across. Yes, sir, ah
think he's goin' to be right in there with us.

CLARENCE
That's not good enough, Floyd. Ah'm meetin' with some
people at the bank tomorrow and ah can't go in there with
a maybe.

FLOYD
What people? Damnit, Clarence, you're not tryin' to drill
around me, are you?

CLARENCE

I'm not tryin' to drill around anybody! Ah'm jest tryin' to get this damn outfit on its feet, that's all.

FLOYD

Ah jest don't like the idea of you meetin' people about this deal without me bein' there.

CLARENCE

Ah didn't include you 'cause you were spozed to be makin' the arrangements about that goddamned military-school business!

MAUREEN

That's right, Floyd, you always bring the barbecue, remember?

CLARENCE

(To FLOYD*)* Can't you shut her up.

FLOYD

Stay outta this, Maureen.

MAUREEN

Stay out, hell! He's gonna git this deal on its feet all right, and one of them feet is going to be right on your neck!

CLARENCE

That's a damn lie. Floyd went into this deal with his eyes wide open. This whole project is split fifty-fifty and don't you forget it! Now listen, Floyd, this outfit is going to go through, but the arrangements have got to be between you and me. *You* and *me*, you understand! So just muzzle that woman you've got over there, and tell her to keep her nose outta this.

FLOYD

Now just wait a minute, Clarence. You by God watch the way you talk about Maureen!

CLARENCE
Then keep her off my back, Floyd!

MARTHA ANN
Boys, boys, this is silly. My goodness, let's not squabble.

MAUREEN
Yeah. Let's not fight about anythin' silly, like old Maureen.
I mean, what the hell?

MARTHA ANN
Ah don't think it's nice to fight. After all, look at all the pretty
things we're goin' to buy after we make all that money.

CLARENCE
Ah wish you'd quit talkin' like we're livin' out on the by-God
poor farm. Hell's fire, you got a house full of "pretty things"
now. *(To* FLOYD*)* Pestered me to death to buy her that
damned sports car over to San Angelo.

MARTHA ANN
Ah just love that little old car, Maureen. Ah call it mah Buzz
Buggy. Ain't that cute?

MAUREEN
Yeah, *cute.*

CLARENCE
Now, Floyd, about that property of the Colonel's . . .

MARTHA ANN
I ain't got a full-length mink coat, though.

CLARENCE
What?

MARTHA ANN
Mavis Purnell's got one.

CLARENCE

Will you please stop harpin' about that goddamned coat. Ah said you couldn't have one and that's that!

FLOYD

Listen, why don't you girls go to a movie or go over to the country club or somethin'. Clarence and I got business to talk about and you-all are jest gittin' in the way.

CLARENCE

(Looking at MAUREEN.*)* That's the damn truth.

MAUREEN

Hey, Martha Ann, how 'bout takin' the Buzz Buggy and whizzin' over to Red Grover's bar. It's spozed to be the hottest spot in town.

FLOYD

You stay outta that goddamned dive!

MAUREEN

How about it, Martha Ann?

MARTHA ANN

Oh no, I'd be scared to go in there.

MAUREEN

Couldn't be any worse than a knee-grabbin', fanny-pinchin' Saturday-night dance out to the country club. Right, Clarence?

CLARENCE

What the hell's that supposed to mean?!

FLOYD

For Christ's sake, Maureen, git off it, will you.

MAUREEN

Okay, okay.

FLOYD
Now, Clarence, like ah was tellin' you. I'm pretty sure that Dad's gonna come across, but I cain't exactly say when. Now, that's the best ah can do.

CLARENCE
Ah don't think so.

FLOYD
Ah'm tellin' you, Clarence, that's how it is.

CLARENCE
Is it? Ah don't know why, Floyd old boy, but for some damn reason you're tryin' to hold out on me.

FLOYD
What the hell you talkin' about?

CLARENCE
You know damn good and well what ah'm talkin' about! Now what is it, you want outta the deal or somethin'?

FLOYD
Out of the deal? No! Ah don't know what you mean.

CLARENCE
Uh-huh. Listen, Floyd, when did you take over your dad's half of the Kinkaid interests?

FLOYD
In 1945. Listen, Clarence, I don't . . .

CLARENCE
And before that your Uncle Brewster handled ever'thin', ain't that so?

FLOYD
Well, yes, but . . .

CLARENCE
Accordin' to Brewster, he had to run things 'cause your dad had some kind of spells after he came back from the war, ain't that right?

FLOYD
Yeah, that's right.

MAUREEN
What the hell you gittin' at, Clarence?

CLARENCE
Floyd doesn't need the Colonel to *give* him a damn thing. Hell, that old man's had snakes in his boots ever since the World's War I. All Floyd does is go down to Judge Deckert and take that piece of property. Ain't that right, Floyd? (FLOYD *doesn't answer.*) Floyd?

FLOYD
Yeah, that's right.

CLARENCE
Uh-huh, and just when did you do that little old thing?

FLOYD
Last week.

MAUREEN
What!

CLARENCE
Ah figured as much. So the truth of the matter is that we got no problems at all.

FLOYD
Yeah, ah reckon so.

MAUREEN
You mean to tell me that you tried to get the Colonel to give you somethin' that you had all along?!

FLOYD
That's not how it is, Maureen. You jest don't understand.

MAUREEN
Oh, I understand all right. I understand the military-school business, I understand Mumford County Estates, oh, brother, do I understand all that, but what I don't understand is you, Floyd, you and your father. My God, I'll never forget the look on that old man's face after his meetin' with that idiot major and after you laid all that Franklin crap on him.

FLOYD
Maureen, please.

MAUREEN
I've stuck by you through a lot, Floyd, but this time you've pushed it too damn far!

CLARENCE
Well, ah think Martha Ann and me better be gittin' on back home.

MAUREEN
Yeah, Clarence, why don't you do that little old thing?

CLARENCE
Ah'll tell those fellas tomorrow that we're ready to go, okay, Floyd?

FLOYD
Sure, sure. All right.

CLARENCE
(Laughing) Now, don't be too hard on him, Maureen. After all, think of all the "pretty things" that you-all are gonna buy.

MAUREEN
You know, Clarence, if bullshit was music, you'd be a by-God brass band.

CLARENCE
(Ruffled, exits.) Come on, Martha Ann!

MARTHA ANN
Well, it shore has been a lovely . . .

CLARENCE
(Offstage) Come on, Martha Ann!!

(She exits.)

FLOYD
(After a pause) Are you going to let me explain?

MAUREEN
Why bother? I just don't give a damn any more.

FLOYD
I wanted Dad to give me something, just *give* me something.

MAUREEN
Seems to me that's all he's ever done.

FLOYD
No, damnit, no, he hasn't. He let me run things 'cause he didn't have no choice in it, but he's never given me anythin'. Ah wanted him to let me have the Genet farm property because he wanted me to have it, wanted to see me do somethin' with it.

MAUREEN
Floyd, he still hasn't *given* it to you. You *took* it from him.

FLOYD

Ah had to. Without that land in mah name, this deal would never have even got off the ground. Ah wanted Dad to think he'd turned it over to me. Ah wanted Clarence and the rest of them fellers to think Dad and me was in on the deal together. Ah can turn that lake property into something, Maureen. Ah know ah can. Ever'body in the whole damn state will be impressed, you'll see.

MAUREEN

Why didn't you tell the Colonel all this?

FLOYD

Ah tried to, but he went off on one of his rampages again. Somethin' about Chinamen or some damn thing. Then we got into a fight as usual and the whole blasted thing went up in smoke.

MAUREEN

But you're worse off now than you've ever been. Now you've got to tell the Colonel that whatever he does, it won't be no use. That property is gone, you've taken it.

FLOYD

Just 'cause ah've taken it don't mean it's gone. Ah mean, what the hell, ah'm not goin' to put it in my pocket and carry it off some place. Jesus, him and his damn ghost town. There never was no town out there, jest some kind of farmin' community, ah looked it up in the courthouse records. Nobody even remembers who lived out there any more. But the Colonel, the Colonel really has got a thing about it. You know, ah thought maybe there was some people buried out on that land, people he knew, and he didn't want the graves disturbed. But ah looked all over and couldn't find no markers of any kind. Hell, ah don't know, maybe ah'd better git ahold of Clarence and tell him to forgit the whole damn thing.

MAUREEN

No, Floyd, don't do that. You need this project, but you've got to tell your dad the truth. You're into it now and you've got to face every part of it.

FLOYD

Yeah, ah guess so. You know we could take a beatin' on this deal. The whole outfit could fall flat on its ass. We could really blow a bundle. That's a hell of a possibility.

MAUREEN

(Sympathetically) I know, Floyd, I know.

(The phone rings.)

FLOYD

Now, who the hell can that be? *(He picks up the phone.)* Hello . . . what . . . damnit to hell, Ramsey-Eyes, talk slower, ah can't understand you . . . What! . . . Oh, Jesus Christ! Now don't you-all move him or anything. Ah'm comin' right on over there. *(He hangs up.)*

MAUREEN

What is it?

FLOYD

It's Dad, he's had another stroke or somethin' down to that damn lodge meeting.

MAUREEN

What?

FLOYD

Ah've got to get into town right away. You call Doc Crowley and tell him to meet us at the hospital. If those stupid bastards at that damn lodge had anythin' to do with this, ah'll have their hides. Ah'll close down that place and kick some goddamn butts, you just see if ah don't. *(He exits.)*

MAUREEN
(Crossing to the phone.) My God, what now?

ACT II

Scene 3

The den. It is late at night. The COLONEL *is stretched out in the armchair. His head is supported by a large pillow. He is wearing pajamas and is covered with a blanket.* MAUREEN *and* FLOYD *sit silently watching him.* CLAUDINE HAMPTON *enters from the bedroom. She is a pleasant, middle-aged woman wearing a white nurse's uniform.*

CLAUDINE
(Talking softly) Well, now, ever'thin's all set up in there for the Colonel, oxygen tent and the works. Looks like a regular hospital room.

FLOYD
Ah'm sorry about all the extra work, Mrs. Hampton, but the Colonel jest wouldn't stay at the hospital. Kept shoutin' that he wanted to come home.

CLAUDINE
Well, ah don't blame him one bit. Poor old man wanted his own house, that's all. Now, you-all go on and git some sleep. I'll watch out for ever'thin'.

MAUREEN
You'll call us if anything happens?

CLAUDINE
Of course, now you go on.

MAUREEN
Come on, Floyd, you've had it, baby.

FLOYD
Maybe ah'd better wait here.

MAUREEN
There's nuthin' you can do, Floyd. Come on now and get some sleep.

FLOYD
Yeah, okay. You be all right, Mrs. Hampton?

CLAUDINE
Shore, shore.

FLOYD
Well, then, good night.

CLAUDINE
Good night. *(They exit.* CLAUDINE *crosses to the* COLONEL. *She checks his pulse, shakes her head, and sighs. There is a quiet knock on the patio door. She crosses over to it and admits* MIKE TREMAINE.*)* Well, howdy there, Mike. Whattayou doin' prowlin' around here this time of night?

MIKE
Olin Potts come by mah place and told me about the Colonel takin' sick and all that. So ah come over as soon as ah could, and ah kindly waited around till the family left.

CLAUDINE
Well, come on in. My goodness, it's a wonder the skeeters didn't eat you alive.

MIKE
Thank you, ma'am. *(Entering.)* How is he?

CLAUDINE
(Shaking her head.) It ain't good, Mike. It ain't good at all. Poor old feller.

MIKE
He oughta be in the hospital.

CLAUDINE
Don't matter where he is any more, Mike.

MIKE
He's a fine man, the Colonel is. A real gentleman.

COLONEL
(Talking in a low voice.) Ah told you, you weren't no good at lyin', Mike Tremaine. What you jest said proves it.

CLAUDINE
Well, now, listen there. How do you feel, Colonel Kinkaid?

COLONEL
Rotten. Where am ah?

CLAUDINE
Why, you're home now, Colonel. Right where you wanted to be. Now ain't that nice?

COLONEL
Who are you?

CLAUDINE
Claudine Hampton, Colonel.

COLONEL
Oh, yeah. You're Skip's mama, ain't you?

CLAUDINE
That's right, Colonel. Mustn't talk too much, you need your rest.

COLONEL
What the hell happened to me? Ah feel weak as a baby. Somebody didn't shoot me, did they?

CLAUDINE
Of course nobody shot you. You're jest tired, that's all, wore out. You need to git a little rest.

COLONEL
Had the damnedest dream. Thought ah was back in the trenches again. Ah could see the Germans comin' up through the wire. It was jest as real as when ah was there.

CLAUDINE
Now, Colonel, ah think it's time you went on into your room. Mike, give me a hand, will you?

MIKE
Shore thing.

COLONEL
No, no, don't do that. Ah'm comfortable. Ah wanna stay here a little longer. Damnit, now keep clear of me, woman.

CLAUDINE
You want me to fetch Floyd and Maureen? They been awful worried about you.

COLONEL
No, leave 'em be. They're probably asleep or somethin'. It's pretty late, ain't it? What time is it?

MIKE
It's two o'clock, Colonel.

COLONEL
In the mornin'?

MIKE
Yes, sir.

CLAUDINE
Colonel, ah really think you oughta . . .

COLONEL
Will you sit down and quit flutterin' around. Worse than a
Red Cross nurse. Flutter, flutter. Actual ever' part of 'em
would flutter but their feet. They had these big shoes on, you
see, and they would stomp. You could hear 'em comin' a mile
away. Stomp, stomp, flutter, flutter.

CLAUDINE
You should be tryin' to conserve your strength, Colonel.

COLONEL
Hell with it! What do ah need to conserve my strength for?
Cain't go fishin', cain't shuffle no dominoes, cain't do a damn
thing. Too damn old. Too damn old for anythin'.

MIKE
Maybe you oughta do what Mrs. Hampton says, Colonel.

COLONEL
No! No, by God, ah won't. Ah am Colonel Jefferson C. Kinkaid, damnit! Officer in the A.E.F. So don't by God tell me
what to do.

CLAUDINE
I'm gonna wake up his folks. *(She exits into the living room.)*

COLONEL
Why the hell am ah so weak? Oh, God, ah ain't gonna die, am
ah?

MIKE
No, Colonel. 'Course you ain't gonna die.

COLONEL
Yes, ah am. Ah know ah am. Ah can feel it. Oh, Jesus, but it's scary, Mike. It's a godawful scary feelin'. Ah'm gonna shut off, just shut off, and slip into nuthin' at all. Rot in the ground like an old dead tree or somethin'. Dead and waxy and drippin' like them bodies ah seen in France. We used to stack 'em up like cord wood on the dead wagons. Now it's my turn. Oh, God in heaven, now it's my turn.

MIKE
Please, Colonel, please don't talk this way.

COLONEL
Ah cain't help it, Mike, ah'm afraid. The death wagon comin', Mike. It's comin' for me. The bells of hell, the bells of hell— ah kin hear 'em ringin'.

*(*FLOYD, MAUREEN, *and* CLAUDINE *enter.)*

CLAUDINE
Your folks are here now, Colonel. *(To* FLOYD*)* Now you jest tell your daddy to stop all this foolishness and let me git him on into bed.

FLOYD
Dad, now you listen to Mrs. Hampton. She knows best.

COLONEL
Don't give a damn if she does. Ah don't want people touchin' me, foolin' around with me, tellin' me not to talk.

MAUREEN
Nobody's gonna touch you, Colonel. You jest stay right where you are. Everything's gonna be all right.

COLONEL
Ah think ah'm fixin' to die.

CLAUDINE
Oh, pshaw now, Colonel. You ain't either.

COLONEL
Things keep comin' into my mind. Long-ago things comin'
back jest as real as real. The trenches, old Carter Tremaine,
Franklin, Elizabeth, Charlie Parsons, and the boys out to the
ranch. Suzette Genet . . . Suzette Genet . . . *(He pauses a
moment.)* Floyd.

FLOYD
Yes, Dad.

COLONEL
You can have that land out there, Floyd.

FLOYD
No, Dad. Please, let's never talk about that any more. That
land's yours.

COLONEL
You take that land and build some houses on it. Let folks get
some use out of it again. There ain't nuthin' left out there for
me nowadays. The things ah seen and remember in this
country is all gone now. Even the sounds of things is gone.
That's right. Even the sounds of things. The creakin' noise
the saddles used to make when we went to work of a mornin',
men yellin', dogs barkin', horses stompin' and snortin' and
fartin' around. A windmill clankin' in the night and cattle
bawlin' from way off yonder some place. Ah can see my
father coilin' up his rope, sittin' on that dun mare of his
straight as a by-God ramrod. Ah recollect Charlie Parsons
and me ridin' across that Seven Spear country on the way to
the Genet place—bein' there with Suzette out by the stock
tank, listenin' to the frogs and talkin' about how things was

gonna be after we got married. How good the lights looked
at the ranch headquarters when you was ridin' in after dark
or goin' out early of a mornin', an' hearin' the deer bump,
bump through the brush. Sometimes, when we'd round up
and corral some of the stock, a few deer would get mixed up
with the bunch. We'd close the corral gate and them damn
deer would jest jump right over the fence. Jump plumb over
the fence and run off while the cattle would jest stand around
lookin' dumb and stupid. Ah liked workin' on the ranch.
Maybe ah should have stayed there 'stead of jumpin' the
fence and runnin' off all over the damned world. The Philippines, Mexico, France—but then if ah hadn't of, ah would
have never got to serve with old Black Jack. By God, that was
somethin' all right. Never would have heard old Harry Truman cuss them mules there in the Herrenberg Forest. Never
would have, never . . . hey, Mike, Mike.

MIKE
Yes, sir.

COLONEL
I'm the oldest livin' graduate of the Mirabeau B. Lamar Military Academy. Ain't that a helluva note. Oldest livin' graduate. Betcha didn't know that . . . did ya?